With Jesus in Jerusalem

With JESUS in JERUSALEM

THE FIRST WAY OF THE CROSS

Étienne Méténier

Our Sunday Visitor
Huntington, Indiana

30 29 28 27 26 25 1 2 3 4 5 6 7 8 9

Our Sunday Visitor Publishing Division
Our Sunday Visitor, Inc., 200 Noll Plaza, Huntington, IN 46750; 1-800-348-2440

ISBN: 978-1-63966-381-1 (Inventory No. T3006)
eISBN: 978-1-63966-382-8
LCCN: 2025945934

Translation: Helena Scott
Cover and interior design: Amanda Falk
Cover art: The 4th Station, in the crypt of the Armenian Catholic Cathedral of Jerusalem (probably built on the foundations of the Byzantine church of Hagia Sophia)

PRINTED IN THE UNITED STATES OF AMERICA

TABLE OF CONTENTS

XII
XIII
X
XI
XIV
IX
VIII
VII
VI
V
I
II
III
IV

INTRODUCTION

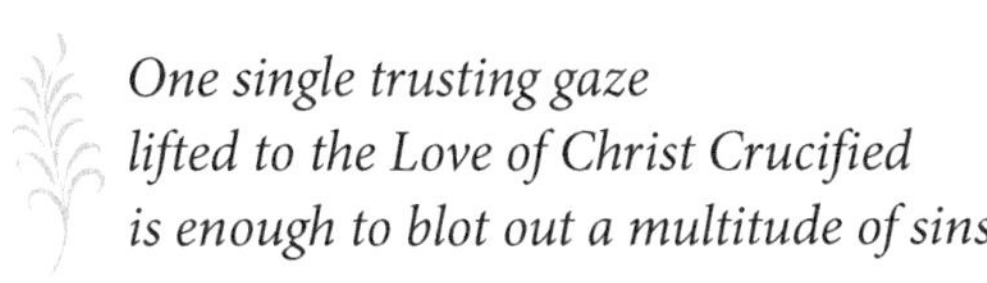

Mary, who was a "specialist" in meditating in her heart on her son's words and deeds (cf. Lk 2:19, 51), probably often called to mind all the events of Good Friday. For about seven years in Jerusalem, until the stoning of Stephen, and then, according to tradition, roughly another seven years in Ephesus, until her dormition, every Sabbath eve she would revisit the holy places, and then the stations that represented them, kept alive in local traditions.[1]

St Francis of Assisi made a pilgrimage to the Holy Land, and to help Christian Europe visualize the events of the Incarnation he brought home with him the devotions of the Angelus prayer, the crib, and the Stations of the Cross, even though their exact form may have evolved over time since then. To him is attributed the brief prayer that follows the announcement of each Station: "We adore you, O Christ, and we bless you, for by your holy Cross you have redeemed the world."

When followed with heartfelt conviction, this centuries-old devotion, so much loved by the saints, is a **fruitful spiritual pilgrimage**. It can obtain the grace to make us grow in love for Christ, gratitude for his passion, repentance for our sins, strength for our spiritual fight,[2] and imitation of his total self-giving. (All of these graces together are synonymous with indulgences,[3] cf. Lk 7:47: "Her sins, which are many, are forgiven, for she loved much.") This devotion can also obtain for us the grace to imitate his unconditional forgiveness through his blood (Rv 1:5), together with acceptance of our own crosses. Contemplating the Passion as we do the Stations of the Cross has the power to inflame the coldest hearts; if our tortured God finds in someone the slightest chink of humility and thirst, he pours into that chink torrents of love, redemption, and communion.

For example, Jesus recommended to **St. Faustina** to do the Stations of the Cross at 3:00 p.m. every day,[4] so that the world could receive his Mercy.[5] **St John Paul II**, from his childhood on (well before Faustina's *Little Journal* was first published in 1981), used to do the Stations of the Cross personally or in public every day in Lent, and at least every Friday during the year, and he had the fourteen stations set up in the papal apartments.

In German, the traditional name for this devotion is *die geistliche Strasse*, "the path of the Spirit," which indicates how it confers the Holy Spirit. If we are closely united to Jesus, it fulfills the Desert Fathers' adage, "Pour out your blood, receive the Spirit."

Because of the infinite merits of Christ's passion, this devotion is a powerful act of intercession for the conversion of sinners, world peace, and the holy souls in purgatory as the result of his victory.

Let us set off to follow Jesus, who "endured the cross, despising the shame, and is seated at the right hand of the throne of God" (Heb 12:2).

"If any man would come after me, let him deny himself and take up his cross and follow me" (Mt 16:24).[6]

"Therefore let us go forth to him outside the camp, bearing abuse for him" (Heb 13:13).

"Come to me, all who labor and are heavy laden, and I will give you rest. Take my yoke upon you, and learn from me; for I am gentle and lowly in heart, and you will find rest for your souls" (Mt 11:28–29).

Where did the Way of the Cross take place? New hypotheses are constantly being presented as the correct one, but they are never conclusive and are regularly replaced by alternatives. The most ancient tradition is that of the Via Dolorosa, situating the tribunal (*bêma*, or judgment-seat, cf. Mt 27:19) or praetorium (Mt 27:27) not at Pilate's personal residence[7] but at the Roman fortress called the Antonia, against the northwest side of the Temple esplanade. It is 830 meters along the narrow, bustling little streets of the souks to Golgotha outside the city.

This path taken by the "Lord of hosts" (1 Sm 1:3) and King of the Universe is like the inversion of the triumphal processions of the Roman generals and emperors with their crowns, rich garments, trophies, corteges, praises, and sacrificial offerings.

Every **Mass** makes present Christ's preaching (the Liturgy of the Word) and his passion and resurrection (Liturgy of the Eucharist). There we can relive the Way of the Cross; we are recommended to use our memory and imagination to re-present it to ourselves — that is, to make the whole thing present.[8] We can console the Beloved, and be his faithful friend in suffering.

In this book each Station of the Cross will be introduced by several verses from the Bible, either relating directly to the event we are meditating on or announcing it, or echoing it according to tradition (especially verses from the Old Testament). Similarly, several aids to meditation will be offered.

During personal or community prayer, readers may select the verse(s) or meditation(s) that best help their focus on a given day, so this book can act as a source for many different meditations on the passion of Jesus.

Other entries are intended to help readers deepen their knowledge of the historical or archaeological background. This, it is hoped, will shed more light on their prayer journey, and add greater depth to it.

Reflection by St Bernard of Clairvaux

Bernard of Clairvaux compares all the Savior's bitter sufferings to a bundle of myrrh which the soul, his beloved, places close to her own heart. "From the moment of my conversion, seeing my lack of virtue, I took this priceless treasure for my own. ... I have experienced how wisdom consists of meditating on these mysteries. They themselves contain

Basilica of the Holy Sepulcher

the perfection of justice, the fullness of knowledge, the riches of salvation, the treasure of merits … there flows from them, sometimes a drink of health-giving bitterness, sometimes an oil of sweet consolation. This is what sustains me in adversity and contents me in prosperity."[9]

Meditations of Anne-Catherine Emmerich

In the neighborhood of her dwelling, behind her house on the mountain-slope, the Blessed Virgin herself set up the holy Way of the Cross. During the whole time she had spent in Jerusalem after the Lord's death, she had not ceased to trace the Via Dolorosa, watering it with her tears. She had measured step by step the distances of all the stations, and her love could not forgo this unceasing contemplation of the Via Dolorosa. From the time of her arrival at Ephesus, she daily went on foot along part of the mountainside, meditating on the mysteries of the Passion. I saw her at first going alone and, after measuring off all the points of the bitter Passion according to the number of steps which she had so often counted, she raised a memorial stone in remembrance of the special suffering there endured by her divine son. If a tree happened to be standing on that particular spot, she marked it as one of the stations. The way led into a neighboring wood, where a slight rise represented Calvary, and a small grotto in the side of another little slope represented the Holy Sepulcher. After all the twelve stations were definitively marked, the Blessed Virgin made the holy Way of the Cross with her maid, in silent meditation. When they reached each station, they sat down and renewed in their hearts the memory of the mysterious sufferings of the Lord, praising him with love and abundant tears. Later on, she improved the arrangement of the stations; I saw her with a sharp instrument, a stylus, recording on each stone what had taken place there and how many steps it was to it. I also saw both of them cleaning the cave representing the sepulcher and making it more suitable for prayer.[10]

1. See also *The Complete Visions of Anne-Catherine Emmerich*, vol. 12 (http://annecatherineemmerich.com/complete_visions/volume_12_from_the_resurrection_of_jesus_christ_to_the_assumption_of_the_most_holy_mary/from-the-resurrection-of-jesus-christ-to-the-assumption-of-the-most-holy-mary-part-4/)

2. Cf. 1 Tm 6:12. The fight is against our passions, the spirit of this world (1 Cor 2:12) and the devil. An ancient Latin prayer says, "By the sign of the Cross deliver us from our enemies, O Lord our God."

3. Scripture and the Church teach that God created us to be responsible and that our good or bad actions have lasting spiritual effects: good actions (such as the Stations of the Cross), each in their own degree, open us up to grace and, in particular, free us from the temporal effects of our sins. Cf. *Directory on Popular Piety and the Liturgy*, no. 132; *Catechism of the Catholic Church*, no. 1471. If accompanied by a sincere confession, holy Communion, and a prayer for the pope's intentions, the Stations of the Cross devotion is granted a plenary indulgence: see the *Enchiridion of Indulgences* (Apostolic Penitentiary, 1999).

4. *Divine Mercy in My Soul*, Notebook 5, 1572.

5. St. Faustina explains: "Jesus told me that I please him best by meditating on his sorrowful passion, and by such meditation much light falls upon my soul. He who wants to learn true humility should reflect upon the passion of Jesus. [This gives a clear understanding of many things one could not comprehend otherwise]" (267). Jesus told her: "My daughter, meditate frequently on the sufferings which I have undergone for your sake, and then nothing of what you suffer for me will seem great to you. You please me most when you meditate on my sorrowful passion. Join your little sufferings to [mine], so that they may have infinite value before my majesty" (1512).

6. As noted on the copyright page, unless stated to the contrary, biblical quotations used in this English version are taken from the Revised Standard Version (Catholic Edition).

7. When he came from his capital, Caesarea Maritima, to Jerusalem, Pilate stayed in a palace built about forty years previously by Herod the Great.

8. Padre Pio, for example, saw Christ coming before the crowd as the priest came out of the sacristy, and climbing little by little up to the altar of Golgotha to die at the elevation, and rise from the dead when a faithful heart devoutly received him in holy Communion.

9. Sermon 43 on *Songs* 1:13.

10. Cf. *Complete Visions of Anne-Catherine Emmerich*, Vol. 12, from the Resurrection of Jesus Christ to the Assumption of the Most Holy Mary, Part 4.

Hour by Hour Chronology of Jesus' Passion

The probable chronology of the Sacred Triduum according to the Synoptic Gospels:

Holy Thursday (April 6, AD 30)

3:00 p.m.	Sacrifice of the lamb for the Jewish Passover
6:30 p.m.	Jewish Passover meal in the cenacle
8:00 p.m.	Descent to the Garden of Olives
8:30 p.m.	Agony in Gethsemane
9:30 p.m.	Kiss of Judas, episode of Malchus' ear, fall into Cedron brook (cf. Ps 110:7), climb back to Mount Sion
10:00 p.m.	False trial before Caiaphas
11:00 p.m.	Thrown into a pit (Ps 88:6)

Good Friday

5:00 a.m.	Taken to the Antonia Fortress (Lk 23:7 says he was also sent to Herod's palace)
5:30 a.m.	False trial, scourged, crowned with

	thorns, condemned to death
7:30 a.m.	The Way of the Cross
9:00 a.m.	Crucifixion
12:00 p.m.	Darkness over the earth at "the sixth hour" (Jn 4:6): the universe in mourning
3:00 p.m.	Death, earthquake, bodies rise from tombs, confession of the centurion Longinus, descent to underworld
4:00 p.m.	Pierced with a spear: "the tenth hour" (cf. Jn 1:39, as explained in the chapter on the 12th Station)
5:00 p.m.	Burial: "the eleventh hour" (Mt 20:6), entry of the souls of the just into paradise (Lk 23:43)

Holy Saturday

	Christ in the Underworld

Sunday

Dawn	Resurrection — that is, forty hours after Christ's death, and the third day on the calendar

STATIONS OF THE CROSS

1. to the Damascus Gate
2. Ethiopian Monastery
3. Coptic Patriarchate
4. Basilica of the Resurrection
5. Saint Veronica
6. Holy Sepulcher
7. Golgotha
8. Church of the Holy Redeemer
9. Our Lady of the Spasm
10. St. Simon of Cyrene
11. Ecce Homo
12. Flagellation
13. Antonia Fortress

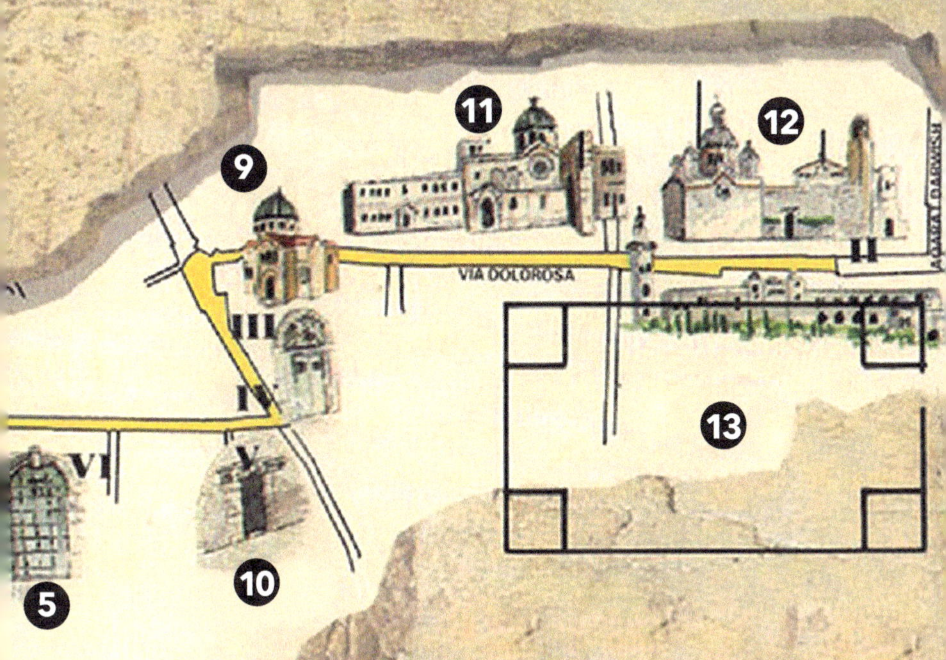

Jerusalem - Via Dolorosa

100 m

Condemned to death: arch of the Ecce Homo Church ("Behold the Man")

1ST STATION

JESUS IS CONDEMNED TO DEATH

We adore you, O Christ, and we bless you,
for by your holy Cross you have redeemed the world.

LET US LISTEN TO GOD'S WORD

From the Gospel According to John

Pilate went out again, and said to them, "See, I am bringing him out to you, that you may know that I find no crime in him." So Jesus came out, wearing the crown of thorns and the purple robe. Pilate said to them, "Here is the man!" When the chief priests and the officers saw him, they cried out, "Crucify him, crucify him!" Pilate said to them, "Take him yourselves and crucify him, for I find no crime in him." The Jews answered him, "We have a law, and by that law he ought to die, because he has made himself the Son of God."

When Pilate heard these words, he was even more afraid; he entered the praetorium again and said to Jesus, "Where are you from?" But Jesus gave no answer. Pilate therefore said to him, "You will not speak to me? Do you not know that I have power to release you, and power to crucify you?" Jesus answered him, "You would have no power over me unless it had been given you from above; therefore he who delivered me to you has the greater sin."

Upon this Pilate sought to release him, but the Jews cried out, "If you release this man, you are not Caesar's friend; everyone who makes himself a king sets himself against Caesar." When Pilate heard these words, he brought Jesus out and sat down on the judgment seat at a place called The Pavement (*lithostrôtos*), and in Hebrew, *Gabbatha*.[1] Now it was the day of Preparation of the Passover; it was about the sixth hour. He said to the Jews, "Here is your King!" They cried out, "Away with him, away with him, crucify him!" Pilate said to them, "Shall I crucify your King?" The chief priests answered, "We have no king but Caesar."

Then he handed him over to them to be crucified (19:4-16).

OPTIONAL MEDITATIONS

- ***"Behold the man!"*** Behold the human being, innocent and holy as he was in the beginning, or as he should be when restored! Behold what the human being is capable of doing through his pride, his anger, his fears, his cowardice and his violence, disfiguring the image of God (cf. Col 1:15), condemning to death the Creator of all life and the divine Judge!

- ***Jesus takes upon himself all your faults***, just as the prophet Nathan reproached David: "You are the man" (2 Sm 12:7).

- ***Men plot their worst against him***, while his only concern is to give up his life to save them. The crowd hate him and howl for his death, while, wounded by their cries, he loves them and wants to give them life, repaying their evil with nothing but good (cf. Ps 38:20).

- ***The Book of Wisdom prophesied***, "Let us condemn him to a shameful death, / for, according to what he says, he will be protected" (2:20). Human folly judges the Judge of the universe; the eternal King is brought before the vain powers of the earth, mockingly draped in a robe with a reed in his all-powerful right hand, the hand that had measured all creation (cf. Is 40:12). He is thus on the point of fulfilling the Scripture of the law of love; but under that crown of thorns is the true God, still more present than in the burning bush (Ex 3). The new Adam lets himself be disfigured by blows, to restore the likeness of Adam (Gn 1:27) deformed by sin.

- ***"He was silent***, because if he had spoken he would have told the Truth, which falsehood is unable to withstand."[2]

- ***Jesus is the true and eternal*** **Bar-Abba**: "Son of the Father." From Jesus' first recorded words, he tells us that he has to be about his Father's business (cf. Lk 2:49). He takes the place of his "brother," the other Barabbas, the criminal who represents all of us sinners, to save us.

- ***This false trial*** and wicked condemnation match and surpass the putting to death of poor innocent Naboth (cf. 1 Kgs 21:13). Rather than being handed over by others, Jesus gives himself up (Jn 10:18 and Is 53:7, Latin: "He offered himself up because it was his will"). And it was really our sins (1 Cor 15:3), much more than the Sanhedrin and Pilate, that spiritually condemned Jesus to death.

LET US PRAY

Let us ask Jesus to forgive us for all our accusations and condemnations:

Every time that we have chosen the accuser of the brethren (cf. Rv 12:10) instead of the merciful Lord (Jas 5:11).
Every time that we have preferred

- our ideologies to the Truth incarnate,
- our fleeting powers to all-powerful Love,
- our fears to confidence in God.

Let us try to accept accusations and condemnations, even unjust ones, with Jesus' patient, unconditional love.

Let us praise him for those who despise him.
Let us follow him for those who reject him.
Let us love him for those who do not love him.

From the sole of the foot even to the head,
there is no soundness in it,
but bruises and sores
and bleeding wounds;
they are not pressed out, or bound up,
or softened with oil.
— Isaiah 1:6

Our Father... Hail Mary... Glory be to the Father...

The crown of thorns

The cap or helmet of thorns, which pierced Jesus' temples and scalp, caused about fifty wounds according to the Shroud of Turin. This "crown" takes on a mocking likeness to the crown of the false god *Sol Invictus* ("unconquered sun") with its rays of light. Later on, the title *Sol Invictus* would also be ascribed to the Roman Emperor.

---

1. *Lithostrôtos* means "paved with stone"; Gabbatha (not actually Hebrew, but Western Aramaic) means "room covered with arches." This was part of the Roman's Antonia Fortress, where the governor could take his seat before a crowd gathered below. This was prior to the rebuilding by Hadrian, which included the arches that can still be seen today in the Ecce Homo convent. A large part of the rocky base on which the fortress was built was covered over with great grooved stone slabs, still visible today, to prevent horses and chariot wheels from skidding.
2. Cf. Ephrem the Syrian, Commentary on the Diatesseron, 20.

The Via Dolorosa in the souk (market) of Jerusalem

2ND STATION

JESUS TAKES UP HIS CROSSS

We adore you, O Christ, and we bless you,
for by your holy Cross you have redeemed the world.

LET US LISTEN TO GOD'S WORD

From the Book of Isaiah

"And the government will be upon his shoulder" (9:6).

"Surely he has borne our griefs
  and carried our sorrows;
yet we esteemed him stricken,
  struck down by God, and afflicted" (53:4).

From the Book of Wisdom

"Blessed is the wood by which righteousness comes" (14:7).

- ***"The symbol of a shameful death***, reserved for the lowest classes" (and which would not even be inflicted on an animal), "the cross becomes a key. From now on, with the help of this key, man will open the door of the deepest mystery of God."[1] According to a classic image, the shameful cross carried by Christ is like the burning candle of the Truth of God's love. By accepting the chalice of his passion the day before, and therefore his cross now, Jesus shows the extent of his love for you.

- ***"There is no wood*** like that of the cross for lighting the fire of love in a soul."[2]

- ***Bernard of Clairvaux*** puts these words into Christ's mouth: "I had, while I bore my cross, a grievous wound, which was more painful than the others and which is not known by men. But reveal it to the Christian faithful and know that whatever grace is requested of me by virtue of this wound will be granted to them. And for all those who honor me for love of this wound, I will forgive them all their venial sins and will no longer remember their mortal sins" (Annals of Clairvaux).

- ***Psalm 95:10 sings***,[3] "*Dominus regnavit a ligno,* the Lord reigns from the wood."

This cross fulfills major types in sacred history:

› the wood carried by the only son (cf. Gn 22:9);
› the doorposts covered in blood that brought salvation (Ex 12:22);
› the rod designating the high priest (Ex 7:9), the mediator dividing the sea (14:16), and, at Marah, turning bitter water into sweet, for the life of the people (15:25); Caesarius of Arles adds, "the cross of Christ transforms the Law";[4]
› the pole from the Valley of Eshcol (Nm 13:23) carried by Israel and the Church between them, sustaining the cluster of grapes for the Blood of Christ;
› the two poles carrying the Ark of the Covenant and of God's presence (Ex 25:15);

› the wooden stick which Elisha used to bring up the piece of iron from the bottom of the River Jordan (2 Kgs 6:1–7), to announce salvation from the weight of our sins;

› the manger that served as a cradle for Christ.

- **Jesus always** "went about doing good and healing" (Acts 10:38), and preeminently so on this path he now treads, in a long procession which will not be the triumphal procession of his enemies, but his own (cf. Col 2:15).

LET US PRAY

Let us accompany Jesus, so that he may heal us.
Let us ask for forgiveness for weighing him and other people down with all our sins and their consequences.

Our Father... Hail Mary... Glory be to the Father...

The Cross of Jesus

According to experimental replicas, in order to support a man of Christ's size, the cross must have weighed about 130 kilograms (286 pounds), being made of roughly hewn Aleppo pine.

There is no proof that what Christ carried was only a *patibulum*[5] weighing about 40 kilograms (88 pounds). The Gospels clearly speak of a cross.

This rough, heavy piece of wood scraped away whatever skin was left on his shoulder (probably down to the bone), arms, and back after the scourging, as witnessed by the Shroud of Turin.

1. Pope John Paul II, Stations of the Cross at the Colosseum, 2000, 2nd Station.
2. Elizabeth of Trinity, Letter 138.
3. In ancient versions, and especially the *Psalterium Romanum*, known to Justin (*Apologia prima*, 41), Augustine (Exp. in Psalm 95), and Ephrem, and taken up in the hymn *Vexilla Regis*.
4. Sermon 201, 1, 22.
5. The crosspiece used for crucifixion. The word means "opening" (from the Latin *patere*): The divine victim's arms were spread out, opened to embrace all mankind.

Close to the ancient stone slabs, Chapel of the Armenians

3RD STATION

JESUS FALLS THE FIRST TIME

We adore you, O Christ, and we bless you,
for by your holy Cross you have redeemed the world.

LET US LISTEN TO GOD'S WORD

From the Book of Psalms:

"But I am a worm, and no man;
scorned by men, and despised by the people.
All who see me mock at me,
they make mouths at me, they wag their heads" (22:6–7).

From the Book of Isaiah:

"Then deep from the earth you shall speak,
from low in the dust your words shall come;
your voice shall come from the ground like the voice of a ghost,

and your speech shall whisper out of the dust" (29:4).

"He was despised and rejected by men;
a man of sorrows, and acquainted with grief;
and as one from whom men hide their faces
he was despised, and we esteemed him not.
Surely, he has borne our griefs
and carried our sorrows;
yet we esteemed him stricken,
struck down by God, and afflicted" (53:3–4).

"All we like sheep have gone astray;
we have turned every one to his own way;
and the Lord has laid on him
the iniquity of us all" (53:6).

Also from the Book of Psalms:

"For he knows our frame;
he remembers that we are dust" (103:14).

"They die and return to their dust" (104:29).

"When thou sendest forth your Spirit, they are created;
and thou renewest the face of the ground" (104:30).

From the Letter of Paul to the Colossians:

"In my flesh I complete what is lacking in Christ's afflictions for the sake of his body, that is, the Church" (1:24).

From the Second Letter of Paul to the Corinthians:

"If we are afflicted, it is for your comfort and salvation" (1:6).

From the Gospel According to Matthew:

"He who does not take his cross and follow me is not worthy of me" (10:38).

OPTIONAL MEDITATIONS

- ***Jesus is only at the start of his* Via Dolorosa**, and already his body gives way and he falls down in our place, he who "upholds all who are falling, / and raises up all who are bowed down" (Ps 145:14). He invites us to follow him, not by choosing but by accepting our crosses (cf. Mk 8:34).

- ***Let us contemplate Jesus' self-abasement,*** in this fall and in the whole of his life. Those who have too much pride in themselves to recognize God's humility stop themselves from truly recognizing God's love, which is proved above all by this humility.

- ***"[Often, souls] do not embrace the cross***, but drag it; [in that way], the cross wounds them, tires them out, and breaks them. But if the cross is loved, it becomes easy to carry" (St. Teresa of Ávila).[1] All the saints have developed Jesus' invitation — Paul (cf. Phil 3:18), John of Ávila (who wrote repeatedly, "You were loved on the cross, so love on the cross"), the Curé of Ars (for whom "worse" than the cross is the fear of the cross). The cross consists mainly of accepting (see Matthew 10:38 in Latin) your own littleness and that of your neighbor.

- ***"Not behind us with the Savior's cross***, but behind the Savior with our own cross" (Cyprian Norwid).[2]

LET US PRAY

Since the Master fell before us, let us no longer refuse to confess each of our falls humbly.

Let us ask Jesus to forgive us for having thrown our own crosses back upon him, and for having thrown him down to the ground by our acts of pride, hardness, contempt, and indifference.

Our Father... Hail Mary... Glory be to the Father...

Dating and historical reliability of these events

If the date of Jesus' passion is calculated in terms of today's calendar, the most probable dating according to most biblical scholars and historians is to place Good Friday on April 7, in the year 30.

The Crucifixion took place the day before a Sabbath (cf. Jn 19:31), which was also the first day of the Jewish Passover, the 15th of the biblical month of Nisan. Over those years, this occurred either on April 7 in the year 30, or on April 3 in the year 33. However, the latter date seems too late for the sequence of subsequent events,

Basilica of the Holy Sepulcher

according to Galatians, the Acts of the Apostles, and other external sources,[3] unless Jesus only began his ministry in the year 30.[4]

Nevertheless, the truth of the events of the Passion and the Resurrection does not depend on the accuracy of this dating.

The Gospels belong to the genre of historical biography (while being highly distinctive, they recount the life, actions, teachings, and even emotions of Jesus Christ, which is far more than simply giving the words of prophets with a few added details). The Gospels were not written according to the principles of modern histo-

riography, which would really be anachronistic, but there are very solid indicators of their reliability, including:

1. The great **diversity of the sources**: Twenty-seven different books of the New Testament, plus the testimonies of subsequent generations and historians, including nonbelievers, on the existence of Jesus and contemporary events. Not even the most powerful and famous men in secular antiquity are recorded in such a wealth

of sources, and very little indeed has been preserved about the lives of rabbis contemporary with Christ.

2. The vast **number of manuscript attestations**: There are over 25,000 manuscripts of the New Testament according to critical editions (including 5,800 in Greek, 10,000 in Latin, and 360 in Syriac), while we have a mere handful of copies, for example, of biographies of Cicero.
3. The **chronological proximity** between the events and their written accounts, which were written down in the decades immediately following, in direct or first-hand testimonies.
4. Minor **contradictions** among the various accounts within an overall convergence: These differences were not erased or harmonized to make them sound more convincing, but reflect the fidelity of what different witnesses perceived, as with any real event.
5. The **uniqueness of these events** in all world history, and the **wisdom** they reveal, which seems utterly impossible for human authors to have imagined.
6. The exponential **growth** of the community of believ-

ers that sprang from the events of Christ's life, despite the weaknesses and divisions of its members and despite severe persecution by its adversaries.

7. The **absence of disagreement** among ancient believers regarding these particular events.
8. The highly convincing **relics** of the Shroud of Turin and the Sudarium of Oviedo.
9. The **lives of the 10,000 saints** and blesseds who recognized Christ's love, and the inner experience of Christ possessed by every believer worthy of the name.
10. The **rational need for God's love** to show itself to humanity through these events, hoping for their free response and that they would let themselves be saved.

---

1. *Conceptos de Amor de Dios*, II, 26.
2. Cyprian Norwid, Polish poet (d. 1883), as quoted by John Paul II in the Stations of the Cross, April 21, 2000, 7th Station.
3. For April 7, A.D. 30, see the *Dictionnaire Jésus*, Laffont, 2021, p. 786.
4. Cf. Jean-Christian Petitfils, *Jésus*, Fayard, 2011.

The 4th Station, in the crypt of the Armenian Catholic Cathedral of Jerusalem (probably built on the foundations of the Byzantine church of Hagia Sophia)

4TH STATION

JESUS MEETS HIS MOTHER

We adore you, O Christ, and we bless you,
for by your holy Cross you have redeemed the world.

LET US LISTEN TO GOD'S WORD

From the Book of Jeremiah:

"You shall say to them this word:
'Let my eyes run down with tears night and day,
and let them not cease,
for the virgin daughter of my people is smitten with a great wound,
with a very grievous blow'" (14:17).

From the Book of Lamentations:

"Is it nothing to you, all you who pass by?

Look and see
if there is any sorrow like my sorrow" (1:12).

From the Gospel According to Luke:

"Do not be afraid, Mary, for you have found favor with God. And behold, you will conceive in your womb and bear a son, and you shall call his name Jesus" (1:30–31).

"He will be great, and will be called the Son of the Most High; and the Lord God will give to him the throne of his father David" (1:32).

OPTIONAL MEDITATIONS

- ***"Mary remembered these words.*** She often returned to them in the secret of her heart. When she met her son on the Way of the Cross, perhaps these very words came to her mind."[1]

- ***"In sin did my mother conceive me"*** (Ps 51:5). Up to the moment of his ascension, the Incarnate Word took our sins upon himself, and at this point we could add, "In sin did my mother see me."

- ***Like Jesus***, everyone who has welcomed the Immaculate Virgin as their mother (cf. Jn 19:27) can testify that when their friends and their own strengths have deserted or betrayed them, Mary still remains with them; they are never alone.

LET US PRAY

Mary, you who lived through the death of your only son, you experienced in the whole of your being what it is to see a loved one suffer:

We commit to you all the sufferings that we bear for those we love.

Mary, all-holy, you are eminently associated with your son's offering for the salvation of the world:

We beg your forgiveness for the sufferings we have

caused you by making your son, Jesus, suffer for our sins.

Jesus, we beg your forgiveness for the sufferings we have caused you through your mother's suffering.

Holy Virgin Mary, you are the one through whom Jesus, our only salvation, was given to us. May the tears you shed for the consequences of our sins preserve us from ever committing any more sins.

Our Father... Hail Mary... Glory be to the Father...

---

1. John Paul II, Stations of the Cross at the Colosseum, April 21, 2000

At the bottom of the hill, formerly the city crossroads.

5TH STATION

SIMON OF CYRENE HELPS JESUS CARRY HIS CROSS

We adore you, O Christ, and we bless you,
for by your holy Cross you have redeemed the world.

LET US LISTEN TO GOD'S WORD

From the Gospel According to Luke:
"And as they led him away, they seized one Simon of Cyrene, who was coming in from the country, and laid on him the cross, to carry it behind Jesus" (23:26).

OPTIONAL MEDITATIONS

- ***Jesus is exhausted*** by the ill-treatment he has already endured and the heavy cross weighing on his shoulders. Humanly, he cannot make it to Golgotha; as God, he chooses to need others, to employ the mediation of others to fulfill his mission.

- ***Requisitioning a random foreigner*** probably suggests that, out of the many people who had received a grace from Christ, not a single one stepped forward at that moment to support him.

- ***Simon shared Christ's cross*** because he was ordered to. We, today, can freely accept suffering and follow the path of charity to relieve Jesus retroactively, and participate in his redemption of the world.

- ***"Simon" means "one who listens"***: The Cyrenian listened to the breathlessness, exhaustion, and sorrow of the one who brings God's breath, the Messiah and Savior. Like the good Samaritan (cf. Lk 10:32–33), he did not pass by "on the other side" of the road. And Jesus' burden is always light (Mt 11:30) in comparison with the eternal salvation he offers us.

LET US PRAY

Let's ask for the grace to be Jesus' Simon of Cyrene. By helping him to carry his cross, I am helping him to save me and to save the whole world.

In response to the invitation in Galatians 6:2, to "bear one another's burdens," let's ask for the grace to be our neighbor's Simon of Cyrene, too: "You did it to me" (Mt 25:40).

Our Father... Hail Mary... Glory be to the Father...

The Uphill Road in Jerusalem

When you follow the Via Dolorosa through the souk in Jerusalem you can see how steep the path taken by Jesus was. With the little strength he had left, it was impossible for him to reach Golgotha unaided.

So, the Romans requisitioned Simon to help Jesus. He was a Jew of the diaspora in Cyrene, in present-day Libya, who had come to Jerusalem to celebrate the Passover.

According to the traditional interpretation of Mark 15:21 and Romans 16:13, this episode was spiritually fruitful, as Simon's son Rufus became a holy disciple in Rome.

Church of St. Veronica (or Church of the Holy Face)

6TH STATION

VERONICA WIPES THE FACE OF JESUS

We adore you, O Christ, and we bless you,
for by your holy Cross you have redeemed the world.

LET US LISTEN TO GOD'S WORD

From the Book of Psalms:

"There are many who say, 'O that we might see some good!
Lift up the light of thy countenance upon us, O LORD!'" (4:6).

"As for me, I shall behold thy face in righteousness;
when I awake, I shall be satisfied with beholding thy form" (17:15).

From the Gospel According to John:

"We wish to see Jesus" (12:21).

OPTIONAL MEDITATIONS

- ***"The fairest of the sons of men"*** (Ps 45:2) and "the image of the invisible God" (Col 1:15), through the blows and spitting of our sins, relinquished all splendor and comeliness (cf. Is 53:2). He accepted being wounded and defiled so that we might be healed and washed clean by his blood and baptism. He longed to behold one day, face-to-face, the beauty of his bride: restored humanity. Veronica's gesture reveals to us the face of the One we long for and will be able to contemplate forever.

- ***Created in the image of God*** (cf. Gn 1:26; Col 1:15), we lost this likeness through sin. God, who revealed himself in his Son, calls us to contemplate and imitate him (1 Cor 11:1) so that this likeness may be restored in us.

- Veronica performed this ***act of compassion*** and, in doing so, contemplated Jesus' passion close at hand.[1] It was this contemplation and this act of charity that restored in her the divine likeness, damaged since original sin.

- ***She lived in humility***, purity, and prayer, aided by the veil which she probably took off to use as a towel, and to which Veronica was able to receive and transmit the image of Christ (known as the Mandylion).

- ***In his Incarnation*** and in the holy icons, Jesus has given us his gaze — sometimes gentle and humble, to console us, sometimes strong and forceful, to educate us.

- ***Like St Thérèse of Lisieux***, let's allow ourselves to be captivated by Christ's face in his passion, through her words: It is "my only homeland, it is my Kingdom of love, it is my smiling meadow, my sweet sun every day" (Poem 20). "O Jesus … we want to wipe your 'gentle face' and console you for the neglect of the wicked; to their eyes, you are still as though hidden" (Prayer 12).

- ***"The soul takes on the likeness*** of what it contemplates perseveringly," says Gregory of Nyssa.[2] Through the prayer of contemplation we allow God to transform us completely, and to inspire and move us to love as he has loved.

- ***Who will give to Christ's holy face*** the kisses that will atone for Judas' kiss of betrayal?

LET US PRAY

Let us ask Jesus for the grace to imitate him in his trust and his charity. Let us ask that his features may be engraved on our hearts, our lives, and the whole of our being.

Our Father... Hail Mary... Glory be to the Father...

Veronica

There is a popular idea that the name "Veronica" means "true image." However, this seems very unlikely.

The tradition that the image of Jesus' face was imprinted on the linen that she used to wipe his face impelled some people to construct a fanciful etymology for her name by joining the Latin *vere*, "true," and the Greek *eikôn*, "image," even though that

Interior of the Church of St. Veronica

meant changing the order of two consonants. In fact, "Veronica" is a Latinized form of the Macedonian name "Berenikê" or "Beronikê," from the Greek *pherein*, "bring," and *nikê*, "victory." So, "Veronica" means "bringer of victory": By her act of charity, faith, and courage she imprinted on herself, and passed on to others, the image of Jesus, who by his passion won the victory over our sins and conquered our reluctance to believe in God's love.

The veil of byssus

The "veil of Veronica," made of byssus ("sea silk," produced by mollusks in the Mediterranean) is said to have been donated by an unknown pilgrim in the sixteenth century to the Monastery of Manoppello in the region of Abruzzi, Italy. In 2006, Pope Benedict XVI went there to celebrate the five hundredth anniversary of the arrival of the veil at Manoppello.

---

1. Cf. John Paul II, Stations of the Cross, 2000.
2. Homily on the Song of Solomon.

7th Station of the Way of the Cross in the Old City of Jerusalem

7TH STATION

JESUS FALLS THE SECOND TIME

We adore you, O Christ, and we bless you,
for by your holy Cross you have redeemed the world.

LET US LISTEN TO GOD'S WORD

From the Book of Psalms:

"Our soul is bowed down to the dust;
our body cleaves to the ground" (44:25).

"What profit is there in my death,
if I go down to the Pit?
Will the dust praise thee?
Will it tell of thy faithfulness?
Hear, O Lord, and be gracious to me!
O Lord, be thou my helper!" (30:9–10).

From the Second Letter of Paul to the Corinthians:

"My grace is sufficient for you, for my power is made perfect in weakness" (12:9).

OPTIONAL MEDITATIONS

- ***He before whom*** "every knee should bow, in heaven and on earth and under the earth" (Phil 2:10) falls to his knees again before us, begging us to accept his merciful love.

- ***The Creator gives way under the heavy cross*** because we give way to the attraction of created things.

- ***Jesus had knelt down earlier,*** in the Cenacle, and continues to kneel here; he who "came not to be served but to serve, and to give his life as a ransom for many" (Mt 20:28).

- ***His blood soaks into the ground***, and the Shroud of Turin shows that his skin has been stripped away from his knees to his shins. Each blow from the cross, each impact against the ground, drives the thorns of our pride deeper into his scalp.

LET US PRAY

Let us keep asking Jesus for forgiveness to the end, despite all the times he has already forgiven us, for having fallen again and again, countless times, for all our refusals to serve him or to serve our neighbor.

As the fruit of his repeated falls, let us ask him for the grace for everyone, never to get used to falling; and to show to anyone who does fall not accusation but compassion.

Our Father… Hail Mary… Glory be to the Father…

Near the former Cardo, or main street, where a Coptic monastery has been built.

8TH STATION

JESUS CONSOLES THE WOMEN OF JERUSALEM

We adore you, O Christ, and we bless you,
for by your holy Cross you have redeemed the world.

LET US LISTEN TO GOD'S WORD

From the Gospel According to Luke:

"And there followed him a great multitude of the people, and of women who bewailed and lamented him. But Jesus turning to them said, 'Daughters of Jerusalem, do not weep for me, but weep for yourselves and for your children. For behold, the days are coming when they will say, "Blessed are the barren, and the wombs that never bore, and the breasts that never nursed!" Then they will begin to say to the mountains, "Fall on us"; and to the hills, "Cover us." For if they do this when the wood is green, what will happen when it is dry?'" (23:27–31).

From the Book of Hosea:

"Return, O Israel, to the Lord your God,
for you have stumbled because of your iniquity" (14:1).

From the Gospel According to Luke:

"[Jerusalem], you did not know the time of your visitation" (19:44).

From the Second Letter of Paul to the Corinthians:

"Blessed be the God and Father of our Lord Jesus Christ, the Father of mercies and God of all comfort, who comforts us in all our affliction, so that we may be able to comfort those who are in any affliction, with the comfort with which we ourselves are comforted by God. For as we share abundantly in Christ's sufferings, so through Christ we share abundantly in comfort too" (1:3–5).

From the Book of Amos

"Seek me and live" (5:4).

From the Book of Jeremiah:

"Then shall the maidens rejoice in the dance,
  and the young men and the old shall be merry.
I will turn their mourning into joy,
  I will comfort them, and give them gladness for sorrow"
(31:13).

OPTIONAL MEDITATIONS

- "***Do not weep*** for him who comes to save those who have faith in him [for he shall rise again as he said], but weep for the impiety of those who are determined to perish" (St. Leo the Great).[1]

- "***Why are you weeping, Mother?*** Instead, cry 'He suffered voluntarily, my son and my God!' [for the salvation of all men]" (Hymn by Romanus the Melodist).[2]

- Apart from John, ***all the men have betrayed him***, denied him, or fled, for different reasons. Women are the witnesses of Christ's passion, and women will be the first witnesses of his resurrection: They carry the life of the body and of the soul, and bear witness to it. Women have been present throughout the Gospel, and they are likewise present in the mission: Tabitha was called a disciple (cf. Acts 9:36), and Junias (Rom 16:7, probably a woman, according to an New American Bible note on the text) is called an apostle in a non-ministerial sense.

- ***Instead of feeling sorry for himself***, Jesus prophesies the sufferings to come upon the people of Israel, sufferings connected to his passion for the redemption of the world (Rom 11:12). He is dying for them, too. Much more than natural tears, what he is hoping for from us are the supernatural tears of repentance.

- ***The only complete consolation*** is the consolation that comes from God, because each Person of the Blessed Trinity is the Paraclete or Consoler (Jn 14:16).

LET US PRAY

Let us ask Jesus for the grace of compassion and consolation for him, and for everyone who suffers, especially those suffering from the worst of all ills — that of not recognizing the Redeemer.

Our Father... Hail Mary... Glory be to the Father...

---

1. Sermon 10 on the Passion.
2. Hymn 25, "Mary at the Foot of the Cross."

The place of the third fall, with Golgotha already in sight.

9TH STATION

JESUS FALLS THE THIRD TIME

We adore you, O Christ, and we bless you,
for by your holy Cross you have redeemed the world.

LET US LISTEN TO GOD'S WORD

From the Book of Psalms:

"[You] lay me in the dust of death" (22:15).

From the Book of Lamentations:

"Let him sit alone in silence
when he has laid it on him;
let him put his mouth in the dust —
there may yet be hope" (3:28–29).

From the Book of Psalms:

"My soul cleaves to the dust;
 revive me according to thy word!" (119:25).

"He raises the poor from the dust,
 and lifts the needy from the ash heap,
to make them sit with princes,
 with the princes of his people" (113:7–8).

From the Gospel According to John:

"Truly, truly, I say to you, unless a grain of wheat falls into the earth and dies, it remains alone; but if it dies, it bears much fruit" (12:24).

OPTIONAL MEDITATIONS

- ***Jesus falls again***, close to the summit of Golgotha, totally exhausted, for us. The Most High falls because of his love for the lowest.

- ***Because he let himself fall*** for our salvation, Jesus conquers the enemy and can say, "I saw Satan fall like lightning from heaven" (Lk 10:18).

- ***Satan strikes at Jesus three times***, making him fall to the ground, because he has in mind his own three falls: at the beginning, during Jesus' earthly life, and at the end of time, according to St. John Henry Newman.[1]

- ***Jesus' falls*** are to raise you up, and to raise up the whole of the universe.

LET US PRAY

Let us ask Jesus to grant us:

- hatred for our sins which, out of indifference or hard-heartedness, cruelly threw him to the ground,
- the grace to get up again (cf. Prv 24:16), as he did for us,
- and humility, so as not to fall into those same sins again (1 Cor 10:12).

Our Father... Hail Mary... Glory be to the Father...

Jesus' three falls

At the third fall, according to the route of the Via Dolorosa, Jesus, who was at the end of his strength, could see the summit of Golgotha, about forty meters (130 feet) away.

Tradition says there were three falls; they symbolize the whole sum of our falls, which Jesus takes on himself.

In the same way, there were three temptations (cf. Mt 4:1–11; 1 Jn 2:16), three denials, and three confessions; and there are three aspersions or immersions in baptism.

All three Persons of the Blessed Trinity are involved in these events.

1. Cf. Stations of the Cross: Meditations for the Via Crucis of the Birmingham Oratory.

Golgotha from outside the basilica

10TH STATION

JESUS IS STRIPPED OF HIS GARMENTS

We adore you, O Christ, and we bless you,
for by your holy Cross you have redeemed the world.

LET US LISTEN TO GOD'S WORD

From the Gospel According to John:

"When the soldiers had crucified Jesus they took his garments and made four parts, one for each soldier; also his tunic. But the tunic was without seam, woven from top to bottom; so they said to one another, 'Let us not tear it, but cast lots for it to see whose it shall be.' This was to fulfill the Scripture,

'They parted my garments among them,
and for my clothing they cast lots.'

So the soldiers did this" (19:23–25).

From the Gospel According to Matthew:

"They offered him wine to drink, mingled with gall; but when he tasted it, he would not drink it" (27:34).

From the Book of Psalms:

"O my God, I cry by day, but thou dost not answer;
and by night, but find no rest" (22:2).

"Dogs are round about me;
a company of evildoers encircle me;
they have pierced my hands and feet—
I can count all my bones—
they stare and gloat over me;
they divide my garments among them,
and for my clothing they cast lots.
But thou, O Lord, be not far off!
O thou my help, hasten to my aid!
Deliver my soul from the sword,
my life from the power of the dog!
Save me from the mouth of the lion,
my afflicted soul from the horns of the wild oxen!" (22:16–21).

"Insults have broken my heart,
so that I am in despair.
I looked for pity, but there was none;
and for comforters, but I found none.
They gave me poison for food,
and for my thirst they gave me vinegar to drink" (69:20–21).

From the Book of Lamentations:

"I have become the laughingstock of all peoples,
the burden of their songs all day long.
He has filled me with bitterness,
he has sated me with wormwood.
He has made my teeth grind on gravel,
and made me cower in ashes;
my soul is bereft of peace,
I have forgotten what happiness is;
so I say, 'Gone is my glory,
and my expectation from the LORD.'
Remember my affliction and my bitterness,
the wormwood and the gall!" (3:14–19).

OPTIONAL MEDITATIONS

- ***The tunic was made of a single piece of cloth***, like the vesture of the high priest, without seams,[1] and John adds a further detail: "woven from top to bottom" (Jn 19:23). Jesus, the one eternal High Priest come from above had prepared himself for the new, definitive sacrifice.

- ***He who clothed the earth*** with plants, flowers, and trees, who clothed the heavens with all the stars, was stripped of his clothes because of our ignominious deeds.

- ***In Genesis 3:21***, Adam was clothed in a tunic made of skins. Today Christ is stripped of his tunic to restore to humanity the innocence lost in Adam. The New Adam is now covered in nothing but the blood from his wounds, as a sign of redemption for the human race (cf. Lv 17:11; Rv 1:5).

- "It was thus [naked] that ***the first man*** dwelt in paradise, and it was thus that the second entered into Paradise" (St Ambrose).[2]

- ***"Jesus delivers us*** from the clothes made of animal skins which Adam wore after his sin. … Jesus had clothed himself in everything that belonged to us, but now we see him stripped of everything so as to strip us of them at the same time as himself" (Pseudo-Athanasius).[3]

- ***"The devil had thrown upon the soul*** the rags of vice, filthy, torn and stinking, and thus made it appear more shameful even than nakedness. … Some men even found their glory in their clothing" (St. John Chrysostom).[4]

- ***Whether Jesus was naked or not***, his passion was, on the human level, ignominious. He accepted it to restore humankind to our original innocence (cf. Gn 3:7). To deliver those who repent from the shame that comes from sin, he took all shame upon himself and "canceled the bond which stood against us" (Col 2:14).

- ***Jesus refuses the sedative drink*** of vinegar and gall (the Roman *posca*) which would dull his awareness during his crucifixion; he cannot accept the fruit of the vine (cf. Is 5:4) where too few people have accepted him.

- ***My people, what have I done to you?*** What do you give me in return for my love? The cross. I gave you manna, you gave me gall; I gave you saving water, you gave me vinegar to drink, according to the the liturgy of Good Friday.[5]

LET US PRAY

Let us ask Jesus, by his merits, at this 10th Station,

- that we may be clothed in the holiness he provided for everyone through baptism,
- for faithfulness, that we may never again take off that garment,
- for the compassion to clothe our neighbor's nakedness (cf. Mt 25:38).

May we quench our Savior's thirst by receiving and sharing in his mercy.

Our Father... Hail Mary... Glory be to the Father...

Reopened Wounds

For the sake of modesty, the *mishna* specified that upon arriving within four cubits of the place of execution, the condemned person should be stripped, but with the front of his body still covered[6] by a loincloth, or *perizonium*.[7]

About two hours after the scourging, the blood all over Jesus' flayed body had already dried, and now, once again, all his skin was torn off. Physically, this must have been one of the most agonizing moments.

Jewish law limited scourging to forty lashes (cf. Dt 25:3), to prevent the victim from dying of loss of blood. The Romans were not so concerned about it: The shroud shows 120 blows from the *flagrum taxilatum* (with lead balls or knucklebones), or 370 visible wounds, some up to six millimeters deep, and probably

600 wounds, if we extrapolate that figure to the sides of the body not visible on the shroud. This was carnage in itself. The bilirubin (showing decomposition of red blood cells) detected on the Shroud testifies, in any case, to extreme suffering, "to the end" (Jn 13:1).

1. Flavius Josephus, *Jewish Antiquities*, 3, 7, 2–161; Philo of Alexandria, *De Fuga*, 110–112.

2. *Treatise on St Luke's Gospel.*

3. *Patrologia Graeca* xxvii, *Expositiones in Psalmos.*

4. *Patrologia Graeca* lxii, 416; 47, 329.340.

5. Cf. *Improperia*, or Reproaches.

6. *Sanhedrin* 6, 3.

7. Cf. the apocryphal "Gospel of Nicodemus," 10, 1. A tradition claims that it is preserved in the reliquary (*Marienschrein*) of the Cathedral of Aix-la-Chapelle, France.

Stairs leading to the summit of Golgotha, Basilica of the Holy Sepulcher

11TH STATION

JESUS IS NAILED TO THE CROSS

We adore you, O Christ, and we bless you,
for by your holy Cross you have redeemed the world.

LET US LISTEN TO GOD'S WORD

From the Book of Psalms:

"[You] lay me in the dust of death. ...
A company of evildoers encircle me;
they have pierced my hands and feet" (22:15–16).

"He committed his cause to the LORD, let him deliver him,
let him rescue him, for he delights in him!" (22:8).

"To thee I lift up my eyes,
O thou who are enthroned in the heavens!" (123:1).

"I stretch out my hands to thee;
my soul thirsts for thee like a parched land" (143:6).

"Hide me in the shadow of thy wings" (17:8).

From the Book of Isaiah:

"He was wounded for our transgressions,
he was bruised for our iniquities;
upon him was the chastisement that made us whole" (53:5).

"By oppression and judgment he was taken away;
and as for his generation, who considered
that he was cut off out of the land of the living,
stricken for the transgression of my people?" (53:8).

"He poured out his soul to death,
and was numbered with the transgressors;
yet he bore the sin of many,
and made intercession for the transgressors" (53:12).

"I spread out my hands all the day" (65:2; cf. also Rom 10:21).

From the Book of Deuteronomy:

"Your life shall hang in doubt before you … you shall be in dread, and have no assurance of your life" (28:66).

From the Book of Zechariah:

"When they look on him whom they have pierced, they shall

mourn for him, as one mourns for an only child, and weep bitterly over him, as one weeps over a firstborn" (12:10).

From Paul's Letter to the Galatians:

"Those who belong to Christ Jesus have crucified the flesh with its passions and desires" (5:24).

OPTIONAL MEDITATIONS

- ***Jewish wisdom*** attributed these figures to the suffering Messiah: the son of Joseph the patriarch, sold by his own brothers.[1]

- ***The Son of God could*** instantly send his legions of angels to overthrow all his torturers and put an end to this inhuman torment by returning to heaven. Yet he allows himself to be stretched out on the wood, to raise you up and lift you toward his Father.

- ***The evil works of our hands*** (cf. Rv 9:20), our steps on the path of iniquity (Wis 5:7), and the perverse thoughts of our hearts (Mk 2:8) inflicted upon him his five wounds. But the new David (1 Sm 17:40) uses them to bring down the evil Goliath and put death to death.

- ***The All-Powerful makes himself completely weak*** and utterly dependent for our sake. Catherine of Siena explains that Jesus was fastened to the cross not by nails, but love.[2]

- ***As Eve stretched out her arm*** for the fruit of original sin, Jesus stretches out his arms to gather salvation for us from his cross. He allows himself to be bound there, so that through his love you may allow yourself to be unbound from your sins.

- ***Instead of Noah*** lying naked in his drunken sleep (cf. Gn 9:21–24), people seek to put Jesus to sleep in death, drunk with love of you on the winepress of the cross.

- ***If Christ had resisted***, he would have killed death instantly, but he first wanted to reveal his love. If he who is the Truth had spoken, he would have immediately silenced error, love would have banished persecution, mercy would have overthrown accusation, praise would have erased blasphemy, and glory would have struck down sacrilege.

- ***By driving in the nails***, the executioners, without knowing it, were firmly and definitively fixing God's infinite love for humanity, which goes so far as to prefer our lives over his own.

- ***He is crucified outside the city*** not only to accomplish the atonement (cf. Lv 16:27), but also to signify that he gives his life for all peoples.

- ***Let us listen*** to what the epistles tell us:

From Paul's Letter to the Philippians:
"[He] emptied himself, taking the form of a servant, being born in the likeness of men. And being found in human form he humbled himself and became obedient unto death, even death on a cross" (2:7–8).

From Paul's Letter to the Ephesians:
"Christ loved us and gave himself up for us, a fragrant offering and sacrifice to God" (5:2).

- ***Jesus stretched out on the cross*** demonstrates the universal invitation of Christ, who desires to embrace all his creatures; the High Priest opens his arms wide to offer the redeeming sacrifice.

- "***The nails fasten the world to God*** and transfix death, the reed writes the faithful into the book of life, the sponge washes the world of its sin, the gall brings forth the sweetness of faith" (Proclus of Constantinople).[3]

- "***These nails*** [like the spear] with which he was pierced have become for me like keys that opened up the treasure of his secrets and let me see the will of the Lord," says Bernard of Clairvaux.[4] Through these wounds, we can see, feel, and taste God, his sweetness, the reconciliation he offers us.

- "***The thief on the left*** and the thief on the right / felt only the nails in the hollow of their hands. / But Christ felt the suffering offered for salvation, / his pierced side, his pierced heart. / And his heart that burned within him, / His heart consumed with love" (Charles Péguy).[5]

- "***He who suspended the earth*** is suspended, he who fixed the heavens is fixed" (Melito of Sardis).[6]

- "***The Word is silent,*** he who heals every sickness and every infirmity is wounded; he is nailed to the tree of the cross to restore to us our right to the tree of life (cf. Gn 3:22)" (Gregory of Nazianzen).[7]

- ***Let us all contemplate the love of Jesus*** raised up on the cross and embracing the universe. May we let ourselves be drawn to him (cf. Jn 12:32) and seduced by him (Jer 20:7).

The more the executioners humiliate him and the more the Lord accepts their offenses against him, the greater his glory grows and the more his love and salvation are manifested.

From the Gospel According to Matthew

"Then will appear the sign of the Son of man in heaven, and then all the tribes of the earth will mourn, and they will see the Son of man coming on the clouds of heaven with power and great glory" (24:30; cf. also Is 11:10).

LET US PRAY

Jesus, we stand before you at this time when you are deserted by your friends and by everyone who received help from you. By our daily conversions, our acts of trust, we want to quench your thirst, warm you, and console you. In your sufferings we see the absolute love that you offer us from this Tree of Life. We never want to turn away from you again. We proclaim that until the end of the world, your cross will no longer be a curse (cf. Gal 3:13), but hope.

Our Father... Hail Mary... Glory be to the Father...

Replicas, based on archaeological data and on the relic on display at the Basilica of the Holy Cross in Jerusalem, Rome.

The nails

Roman carpentry nails were real forged bolts, over a centimeter thick, increasing the Lord's bleeding, and thus his weakness, thirst, and cold.

Even the most amateur handyman knows that nails must be blunted to avoid splitting wood; therefore, our Savior's flesh was crushed as much as pierced, before being stretched for six hours under the weight of his body.

The dislocation of the bones (cf. Ps 22:14) of the carpus and the tarsus, and the piercing of the nerves, made this mode of execution an unspeakable torture.[8]

Nails of this kind go through a wooden beam (perhaps a reused one) more easily if it has predrilled holes, and that could require the nail tips to be hammered down on the other side (as seen on the bone discovered by archaeologists at Giv'at HaMivtar). Several mystics (including Anne Catherine Emmerich and Josefa Menéndez) described the executioners brutally flipping over the heavy cross, with Jesus already fixed to it, face to the ground: giving the kiss of peace to the world he loved so deeply.

When the cross was raised upright, the body of Jesus was fully suspended, with all its weight on his wounds. Driving the cross into the hole cut into the rock at the summit of Golgotha caused yet more jolts.

Once the cross was in place, after so many wounds, instead of pity and compassion there came yet more mockery and insults from men (cf. Mt 27:41–44).

The third hour and the sixth hour

The third hour (9:00 a.m.) is, in the Talmud (*Sanhedrin* 38b), the hour when Adam was, literally, "stretched" from the clay, just as Jesus is now stretched on the wood; mystics confirm that the soldiers pulled hard on his arms.

At the sixth hour, darkness falls upon the earth: It is the hour when Abraham received the three divine visitors (cf. Gn 18), when the sons of Jacob were reconciled (Gn 43:16), when the weary Jesus met the Samaritan woman to convert her (Jn 4), when the Gospel was opened to the pagans (Acts 10:9), when Paul was enveloped in bright light (Acts 22:6), when the beloved of the Song of Solomon wandered and called out to the one her heart loved (Song 1:7). Likewise, the dark cloud of Sinai (Ex 20:21) was the place of God's presence, before the giving of the first Torah.

1. Cf. Talmud *Sukka* 52a.
2. Prayer 13.
3. *Patrologia Graeca* 65, 785.
4. Cf. *Sermons on the Song of Solomon*, 61 and 64.
5. *The Mystery of the Charity of Joan of Arc*, 1910.
6. *On Easter*.
7. Discourse 29, 21.
8. Cicero described it as the worst possible punishment, and Seneca said suicide would be preferable (*Epistulae Morales*, 101). In sacred art it was several centuries before the grace of the Resurrection healed this trauma and enabled the Crucifixion to be represented (the *Holy Face* of Lucca and the *Batlló Majesty*), and further centuries before his wounds were depicted with any realism.

Summit of Golgotha

12TH STATION

JESUS DIES ON THE CROSS

We adore you, O Christ, and we bless you,
for by your holy Cross you have redeemed the world.

LET US LISTEN TO GOD'S WORD

From the Second Book of Samuel:

"O my son Absalom, my son, my son Absalom! Would I had died instead of you, O Absalom, my son, my son!" (18:33).

From the Gospel According to Matthew:

"And behold, the curtain of the temple was torn in two, from top to bottom; and the earth shook, and the rocks were split; the tombs also were opened, and many bodies of the saints who had fallen asleep were raised, and coming out of the tombs after his resurrection they went into the holy city and appeared to many. When the centurion and those who were with him, keeping watch over Jesus, saw the earthquake and what took place, they were filled with awe, and said, 'Truly this was the Son of God!'" (27:51–54).

From the Gospel According to John:

"Since it was the day of Preparation, in order to prevent the bodies from remaining on the cross on the sabbath (for that sabbath was a high day), the Jews asked Pilate that their legs might be broken, and that they might be taken away. So the soldiers came and broke the legs of the first, and of the other who had been crucified with him; but when they came to Jesus and saw that he was already dead, they did not break his legs. But one of the soldiers pierced his side with a spear, and at once there came out blood and water. He who saw it has borne witness — his testimony is true, and he knows that he tells the truth — that you also may believe" (19:31–35).

From Paul's Letter to the Ephesians:

"[Christ reconciled] us both to God in one body through the cross, thereby bringing the hostility to an end" (2:16).

From Paul's Letter to the Colossians:

"Making peace by the blood of his cross" (1:20).

"The bond which stood against us with its legal demands, this he set aside, nailing it to the cross" (2:14).

From Paul's Letter to the Romans:

"But God shows his love for us in that while we were yet sinners Christ died for us" (5:8).

From Paul's First Letter to the Corinthians:

"We preach Christ crucified, a stumbling block to Jews and folly to Gentiles" (1:23).

From Paul's Letter to the Galatians:

"Far be it from me to glory except in the cross of our Lord Jesus Christ" (6:14).

From the Letter to the Hebrews:

"[Christ the High Priest] entered once for all into the Holy Place, taking not the blood of goats and calves but his own blood, thus securing an eternal redemption" (9:12).

OPTIONAL MEDITATIONS

- ***He who breathed into man's nostrils the breath of life*** now breathes his last. Jesus "gives up the Spirit": It is the beginning of Pentecost for those who believe in this "great love" (Eph 2:4) and are grateful. Christ has loved us and given himself up for us (cf. Gal 2:20); he could not find anything more precious to give us, so that we might freely begin to love him and turn to him.

- ***The death of Jesus*** is the supreme stumbling block, the scandal that arouses the envy of Satan and of the world after him: God makes himself weak, to the extreme of dying covered in spittle, reviled, nailed to a plank; and that self-abasement does not reduce his greatness in the slightest, but exalts it!

- ***By being the first to die***, he shows that he has chosen to become the weakest: God has a special weakness for every human being, and for you.

- ***The all-powerful has made himself into all-weakness***. He is *victor quia victima* ("victor because a victim"), in the words of Saint Augustine. Nothing could attract people more powerfully: He is the first one to die for love of his enemies, he is the victor over the evil in all of us by his supreme goodness, he sleeps so that we may wake up.

- ***Because of this testimony*** of sheer love, and not because of miracles, the pagan centurion cries out, "Truly this man was the Son of God!" (Mk 15:39).

- "***Jonah being swallowed by a whale*** was natural, normal; but for Jonah to be alive in the belly of the monster, that was the miracle. Likewise, Christ proved his divinity better by triumphing over death from within the bosom of death than he would have by refusing to die" (John Chrysostom).[1]

- "***He ascended the cross*** by his will; he triumphed upon it by his power; he gathered its fruit by his love" (Guerric of Igny).[2]

- "***There is no cross of ours*** that his body does not feel. Not a single one of our sins that does not leave a wound on him" (Paul Claudel).[3]

- ***Adam hid*** "in the tree" (Gn 3:8, singular in the Hebrew) after his sin; and by a magnificent substitution the new Adam raised upon the tree brings us grace.

- ***This wooden cross has become the standard*** for the nations (cf. Is 11:10–12) of divine Wisdom and Love to the utmost, hence …

  › the **trellis** of "the true vine" (Jn 15:1),
  › the divine **authority** for victory (Ex 17:9; cf. Eusebius),[4]
  › the divine **scourge** against Satan (cf. John Damascene),[5]
  › the **crook** of the sheep of the Good Shepherd (Ps

23:4; Jn 10),

› the **setting** of all the virtues (cf. Thomas Aquinas),[6]
› the **heart** of preaching (1 Cor 1:23),
› the **framework** supporting the Church,
› the **anchor** of salvation,
› the **crane** to lift the stones of the spiritual temple (Ignatius of Antioch:[7] with the cable of the Spirit),
› the **plow** for the field of hearts (Theoleptus of Philadelphia),[8]
› the **support** of all the weary (Ambrose),[9]
› the **nuptial bed** of Christ (Augustine),
› the **bridge** over death (Ephrem),[10]
› the **raft** of the shipwrecked (Romanus the Melodist),[11]
› the **ladder** to heaven (cf. Paulinus of Nola),[12]
› the **mast** to bring souls to safe harbor (cf. Maximus of Turin,[13] also evoking Ulysses bound),
› the **axis** of the universe (cf. Carthusian motto),
› the **gallows** of **condemnation** [and the death of

death] (cf. Maximus the Confessor),

› the shady **foliage** for eternal rest (cf. Hippolytus of Rome).[14]

- ***This cross has been for 2,000 years***, and will be until the second coming of Christ, "a stumbling block to Jews and folly to Gentiles" (1 Cor 1:23), the object of insult and contempt towards Alexamenos (see page 128) and all Christians, to the extreme of martyrdom, but also the object of profanation by those who wear it out of ostentation and deny it by their deeds.

- It is the **palimpsest** where death had been written; Christ's blood has blotted out the document of our debt (cf. Eph 1:14), and by the Resurrection all of it is changed into a glorious book.

- It is the **compendium** of wisdom and eternal knowledge: conversion, gratitude, adoration, charity …

- "***The cross consecrates kings***, adorns priests, protects virgins, strengthens ascetics, tightens the marriage bond of spouses, fortifies widows, makes the Church fruitful, enlightens nations, guards the desert, and opens paradise" (Proclus of Constantinople).[15]

- ***Bernard of Clairvaux*** explains how Jesus in his mortal flesh, having taken the appearance of sin (Rom 8:3; cf. also Nm 21), fulfills the figure of Jacob who took the appearance of Esau (with the animal skin, associated with sin), thanks to his mother Rebekah, a figure of Mary, and was recognized for what he truly was through his voice, by Isaac, as by the centurion.[16]

- ***The Lord's death*** for our sins is accompanied by extraordinary signs, theophanic signs like the ones on Mount Sinai (Ex 19:18; Ps 18:11–14) and eschatological signs (Jl 2:10).

- ***The sun is darkened in mourning*** for its Creator, and creation protests, weeps, and acclaims the Savior all at the same time. Men have denied him or stopped proclaiming him, so the stones cry out (Lk 19:40). They show the unique and universal reach of the greatest drama in history, as in the earthquake on the lake (Mt 8:24, in the Greek), the shaking of the town on Palm Sunday (Mt 21:10, also in the Greek), and afterward at the Resurrection (Mt 28:2) and at the second coming of Christ, the Parousia (Mt 24:7, 29).

- ***These cosmic signs*** had been foretold:

In the Book of Isaiah:
"I clothe the heavens with blackness,
 and make sackcloth their covering" (50:3).

In the Book of Zephaniah:
"A day of wrath is that day,
 a day of distress and anguish,
a day of ruin and devastation,
 a day of darkness and gloom,
a day of clouds and thick darkness" (1:15).

In the Book of Amos:
"Shall not the land tremble on this account,
 and every one mourn who dwells in it,
and all of it rise like the Nile,
 and be tossed about and sink again, like the Nile of Egypt?
'And on that day,' says the Lord God,
 'I will make the sun go down at noon,
 and darken the earth in broad daylight'" (8:8–9).

In the Gospel According to Matthew:
"God is able from these stones to raise up children to Abraham" (3:9).

These signs are not only apocalyptic, but also parenetic:[17] they show what should happen in the heart of someone who contemplates the Lord's passion. While the sun is darkened, we are consumed with a desire to shine; while rocks are split, we harden our hearts.[18]

- ***"Let human nature tremble*** before the suffering of the Redeemer, let the stones of unfaithful hearts be split, and let those who were imprisoned in the tombs of their mortality come forth, lifting the stone that lay upon them" (Leo the Great).[19]

- "*The sun hides its face*, unable to look at the Sun of justice so mistreated (cf. Mal 4:2); the earth shakes, sprinkled with the blood of the Lord, purified of idolatry and trembling for joy of salvation" (Epiphanius).[20]

- ***The veil of the Temple is torn***, and "the angel tears his garments as a sign of mourning" (Melito).[21] God the Father himself, who dwelled in the Sanctuary, goes into mourning for his Son (cf. Gn 37:34). The Syriac text indicates that even the very façade of the Temple was split: this was no mere tremor. And since the Temple veil is torn from top to bottom, it is left wide open: Sinners and pagans now have full hope (Heb 6:19) of access to the sanctuary.

From the Book of Zechariah:

"On that day there shall be a fountain opened for the house of David and the inhabitants of Jerusalem to cleanse them from sin and uncleanness.

And on that day, says the LORD of hosts, I will cut off the names of the idols from the land, so that they shall be remembered no more." (13:1–2)

"'Awake, O sword, against my shepherd,
against the man who stands next to me,'
says the Lord of hosts.
'Strike the shepherd, that the sheep may be scattered;
I will turn my hand against the little ones'" (13:7).

- ***Anyone who claimed*** "I am innocent of this death, it was other people who put him to death," cannot believe in Christ. In fact it would prove that they did not believe. Because believing in Christ means being heartbroken (cf. Cardinal Jean-Marie Lustiger).[22]

- ***Let us contemplate every day*** the "love of Christ which surpasses knowledge" (Eph 3:19), the mystery of the love that saves us.

- ***We have denied*** the One who acknowledged us, mocked the One whose power created us, dishonored the One who honored us with salvation, humiliated the One who exalted us by adopting us, scorned the One who raised us up, rejected the One who called us, condemned the One who forgave us, attacked the life of the One who is Life, killed the One who gave us life.

- ***When a woman gives birth*** (as Jesus says in John 16:21) she is not paying a price for the new life with her labor pains, but giving life value; and likewise Christ in his passion is not paying anyone for our salvation, but giving it even more value. He is giving his divine life.

- ***Even without men's sins***, God loved us so much that he wished to go to the lengths of giving himself totally, even if it meant dying the hardest possible death. Since he, our good, innocent Creator God, died for us, let us, too, live first for him, even to the point of dying for him if necessary. Otherwise, would we not be unfaithful, treacherous, ungrateful, disloyal? More than being understood

or imagined, this unique love deserves to be adored, returned, and imitated.[23]

Alexamenos, a derided Christian

The Alexamenos graffito is a drawing discovered in the nineteenth century on a wall of the imperial palace in Rome and dated between the first and third centuries. This caricature is one of the earliest known depictions of the Crucifixion. Jesus is shown with the head of a donkey, which was the Romans' way of mocking the God of the Jews. Alexamenos is thought to be the worshiper depicted at the foot of the cross, and the inscription beneath the drawing mocks him: "Alexamenos worships God."

LET US PRAY

Jesus, abandoned, we remain at your feet.
We let ourselves be looked at by you.
We entrust ourselves to you.

We let the earthquake shake our indifferent hearts and our sluggish wills.

We proclaim you to be the Son of God.

Grant us the grace of repentance, strength in trials, gratitude and adoration, imitation of you by accepting our own crosses.

Grant us the grace of dying to our sins, of forgiving and loving unconditionally, and without our love being returned.

Our Father... Hail Mary... Glory be to the Father...

A crucified Messiah and ancient heroism

This death, filled with anguish and torment, seems far removed from the heroism of the Maccabees or Greco-Roman martyrs. Neither does its power lie in deliberate imperturbability or calculated glory, which would be purely human attitudes, incapable of carrying conviction; it lies in the fulfilment of Divine Love to the end (cf. Jn 13:1), which abases itself and takes everything upon itself, revealing "what no eye has seen, nor ear heard, / nor the heart of man conceived, / what God has prepared" (1 Cor 2:9), and convincing the hearts of the poor until the end of the world.

The ninth hour and the tenth hour

The ninth hour, according to Jewish tradition, was the hour of the giving of the commandment not to eat from the fruit of the tree (cf. *Sanhedrin* 38b), the hour of the bronze serpent, which also took place on a Friday (*Genesis Rabbah* 9, 14 on Nm 11), the hour of the sacrifice of Isaac (*Shabbat* 89a), after he had carried the wood (Gn 22:6), the hour of the slaughtering of the Passover lamb (Ex 12:6, according to the majority Jewish interpretation), and the hour when Peter and John went up to the Temple for the healing of the cripple (Acts 3:1).

The piercing of the Lord's heart with a spear takes place around the tenth hour, the hour of Adam's sin on the sixth day (*Sanhedrin* 38b), and the hour of Jesus' invitation inaugurating his mission: "Come and see" (Jn 1:39), thus announcing where to meet him; within his own opened heart! Eve had been created from the side of Adam (cf. Gn 2:21), and the Church is born from the side of the New Adam. The sword of the cherubim had barred us from paradise (Gn 3:24), and the spear of the Roman soldier Longinus gives us access to it once more. Christ our rock (Ex 17:6; 1 Cor 10:4) now gives drink to the whole world; the gate of the Temple, now open (Ez 47), brings life even to the driest places on earth.

---

1. 4th homily on 1 Corinthians.
2. Sermon 2 for Palm Sunday, cf. Song 7:9.
3. *Le Chemin de Croix.*
4. Life of Constantine.
5. *De fide orthodoxa* 4, 11.
6. On the Credo.
7. Letter to the Ephesians 8:1.
8. Speech.
9. On Psalm 118.
10. Homily on Our Lord.
11. *Sources Chrétiennes* no. 128, 285.
12. Hymn.
13. *Corpus Christianorum Series Latina* 23, 149.
14. Treatise on Easter, 69.
15. Sermon on Palm Sunday, *Patrologia Graeca* lxii, 772.
16. Sermon on the Song of Solomon, 28, 2.
17. Parenetic: something that provides advice, counsel, or encouragement, especially in a religious or ethical context.
18. Cf. William of Saint-Thierry, Meditative Prayer, V.
19. Sermon 66, 3.
20. *Patrologia Graeca* xliii, 440.
21. Homily on Easter, 98.
22. *Le Choix de Dieu*, 1987.
23. Cf. St. Francis de Sales, Sermons, February 27 and Good Friday, 1622.

The Stone of Anointing

13TH STATION

THE BODY OF JESUS IS TAKEN DOWN FROM THE CROSS

We adore you, O Christ, and we bless you,
for by your holy Cross you have redeemed the world.

LET US LISTEN TO GOD'S WORD

From the Gospel According to Luke:

"Simeon blessed them and said to Mary his mother,
'Behold, this child is set for the fall and rising of many in Israel,
and for a sign that is spoken against
(and a sword will pierce through your own soul also),
that thoughts out of many hearts may be revealed'" (2:34–35).

"His mother kept all these things in her heart" (2:51).

From the Book of Jeremiah:

"A voice is heard in Ramah,
  lamentation and bitter weeping.
Rachel is weeping for her children;
  she refuses to be comforted for her children,
  because they are not" (31:15; cf. also Mt 2:18).

From the Book of Sirach:

"With all your heart honor your father,
  and do not forget the birth pangs of your mother" (7:27).

OPTIONAL MEDITATIONS

- ***The body of Jesus is "unfastened"*** from the cross so that from now on we may "fasten" ourselves completely to him.

- ***Mary receives her son*** after he was taken down from the cross as she received him into her womb at the Annunciation, and into her arms at his Nativity, relying on nothing except God's Word. She who is without sin gave her baby to us in the manger. We sinners return him to her, dead, on Calvary.

- ***God the Father receives Jesus' soul***, and his mother receives his body. They experience the worst suffering in nature: the death of their own child. Unsurpassed suffering, born of unsurpassed love. What more unspeakable sorrow could there be than to see the long, drawn-out torture ending in the death of the Beloved, and to receive him, dead, into one's arms?

- ***The all-loving mother***, the Pietà, receives her dead son upon her lap. What does she do? She embraces him, wipes his wounds with her own robe, and pulls out the sharp thorns of his crown with her fingers, wounding her own flesh, too, for us.

- ***Mary is black*** (with mourning), but beautiful, through her love (cf. Song 1:5 in the NABRE). For about three hours, she sorrowfully keeps vigil over the body of her only son.

- “***Mary endured the death of her heart*** out of such charity that there will never be anything like it again” (Bernard of Clairvaux).[1]

- “***Mary is the shroud and the ointment***, she is the tomb and the myrrh. She is the priest and the altar and the vessel and the Upper Room” (Paul Claudel).[2]

- ***Gregory of Nazianzen has Mary say***: “O precious hand, that I have so often held in mine, to which I have clung like ivy to oak branches! O beloved gaze, O beloved mouth, O face and countenance of my son! O sweetest kiss, O divine body, O most fragrant breath of my son! O perfume whose aroma is divine! In my afflictions I saw you, and my heart was comforted. Why have you chosen to die such a shameful death? Why have you abandoned the mother who bore you? Alas, would that I might die with you, my child! I would rather die than look upon you dead! How can I receive comfort from that silent mouth, from those closed eyes? How can I survive you? O sweet scent of your body! Was it for nothing that my breast nourished you in your swaddling clothes, my child? Was it for nothing that I toiled and exhausted myself in pain, from the very first moments of your miraculous birth? But what sufferings you have given to my heart during your life, and what sorrows since your descent into the underworld, O Son of the Almighty!"[3]

- "***Mary gave birth without pain*** to the author of salvation (Is 66:7–9). . . . Now, at the foot of the cross, she gives birth in great suffering, according to the prophecy (Lk 2:35). Because she truly experienced the pains of childbirth in the passion of her only son, the Blessed Virgin gave birth to our salvation; she is therefore the mother of each one of us" (Rupert of Deutz).[4]

"*I am very dark, but comely*" (Song 1:5)

On the Issenheim Altarpiece, Grünewald depicted Mary enveloped in darkness; she enters with her son into the sleep of Holy Saturday, until the awakening of the "first-born from the dead" (Col 1:18).

LET US PRAY

Stabat Mater[5]

At the cross her station keeping,
Stood the mournful Mother
weeping
Close to Jesus to the last.
Through her heart, his sorrow
sharing,
All his bitter anguish bearing,
Now at length the sword has
passed.

O how sad and sore distressed,
Was that Mother highly blest
Of the sole begotten One!
Christ above in torment hangs,
She beneath beholds the pangs
Of her dying, glorious Son.

Is there one who would not
weep,
Whelmed in miseries so deep
Christ's dear Mother to behold?
Can the human heart refrain
From partaking in her pain
In that Mother's pain untold?

Bruised, derided, cursed, defiled,
She beheld her tender Child,
All with bloody scourges rent.
For the sins of his own nation
Saw him hang in desolation

Till his spirit forth he sent.

O dear Mother! Font of love,
Touch my spirit from above,
Make my heart with yours
accord.
Make me feel as you have felt;
Make my soul to glow and melt
With the love of Christ, my Lord.

Holy Mother, pierce me through,
In my heart each wound renew
Of my Savior crucified.
Let me share with you his pain,
Who for all my sins was slain,
Who for me in torment died.

Let me mingle tears with you,
Mourning him who mourned
for me,
All the days that I may live.
By the Cross with you to stay,
There with you to weep and pray,
Is all I ask of you to give.

Virgin of all virgins blest,
Listen to my fond request:
Let me share your grief divine;
Let me, to my latest breath,
In my body bear the death
Of that dying Son of yours.

Wounded with his every wound,
Steep my soul till it has swooned,
In his very blood away;
Be to me, O Virgin, nigh,
Lest in flames I burn and die,
In his awful Judgment day.

Christ, when you shall call me
hence,
Be your Mother my defense,

Be your Cross my victory;
While my body here decays,
May my soul your goodness
praise,
Safe in Paradise with you.

Our Father… Hail Mary… Glory be to the Father…

---

1. Sermon for the Octave of the Assumption, 15.
2. *Chemin de Croix*. Thirteenth Station.
3. Christ's Passion, 235.
4. On the Gospel of John, 13.
5. Thirteenth-century poem attributed to Jacopone da Todi, OFM. Translation: Edward Caswall.

Interior of the Holy Sepulcher

14TH STATION

THE BODY OF JESUS IS LAID IN THE TOMB

We adore you, O Christ, and we bless you,
for by your holy Cross you have redeemed the world.

LET US LISTEN TO GOD'S WORD

From the Gospel According to John:

"After this Joseph of Arimathea, who was a disciple of Jesus, but secretly, for fear of the Jews, asked Pilate that he might take away the body of Jesus, and Pilate gave him leave. So he came and took away his body. Nicodemus also, who had at first come to him by night, came bringing a mixture of myrrh and aloes, about a hundred pounds' weight. They took the body of Jesus, and bound it in linen cloths with the spices, as is the burial custom of the Jews. Now in the place where he was crucified there was a garden, and in the garden a new tomb where no one had ever been laid. So because of the Jewish day of Preparation, as the tomb was close at hand, they laid Jesus there" (19:38–42).

From the Book of Genesis:

"Judah … couched as a lion … who dares rouse him up?" (49:9).

From the Book of Psalms:

"Thou who hast made me see many sore troubles
  wilt revive me again;
from the depths of the earth
  thou wilt bring me up again" (71:20).

From the Song of Solomon:

"Until the day breathes
  and the shadows flee,
I will [hasten] to the mountain of myrrh
  and the hill of frankincense" (4:6).

OPTIONAL MEDITATIONS

- ***At the beginning of the Gospel we have Mary and Joseph***, and to parallel this, we find Mary and another Joseph at the end. The first Joseph was righteous in not maligning Mary, and received Jesus as he entered human life, wrapping him in swaddling clothes in a cave. The second Joseph was also righteous (cf. Lk 23:50), who received him after he had given his life for us, wrapping him in a shroud in a tomb.

- ***The Son of God came into the world*** emptied, stripped of everything (Phil 2:7), and he leaves it stripped of everything, with not even a tomb of his own. He entered a virgin's womb, and he leaves through a virginal sepulcher, as befits the holiness of the immaculate, sacrificed Lamb. He who fills the universe allows himself to be enclosed in a tomb.

- ***He who took upon himself*** the consequences of all our sins (Mt 8:17) is covered with a shroud, for he covers the earth with his forgiveness. He is buried so that, "buried with him by our baptism" (Rom 6:4), we may die to sin and bury all our passions.

- "***The Passion ends*** and the Compassion continues. … Here ends the Cross and begins the Tabernacle" (Paul Claudel).[1]

- ***Nicodemus, who once came to Jesus*** by night to speak of being "born again," receives the key to understanding the entire paschal mystery of Jesus, out of love for the world (Jn 3:16).

- They unfasten the ***One who has set the whole world free***; they receive the body of the One whose Incarnation so many have rejected; they embrace the One to whom all of us (cf. Rom 3:23) have given a kiss of treachery (Lk 22:47); they bury the Rock of Israel (2 Sm 22:2; 1 Cor 10:4) in the rock; they veil for three days the One whom God came to reveal; they wrap in a burial cloth the One who is the source of all life; they cover with a shroud the One who suffered for our salvation till he was covered in sweat, with a napkin like the one that was wrapped round the wicked servant's coin (Lk 19:20), taking all our iniquities upon himself, even to the depths of the earth.

- ***Joseph and Nicodemus*** sow in the earth the dead grain (cf. Jn 12:24) of the Bread of Life, which, transformed, will not remain alone, but will give the best of all fruits to those who receive and follow him: eternal life. Having passed through the wood of the manger and of the cross, the shoot of Jesse is planted one last time in the earth, for eternal fruitfulness.

- ***Contemplating the boldness*** of Joseph of Arimathea (Mk 15:43), who renounces worldly honors to stand up for Christ at his darkest hour, St. Josemaría Escríva offers this prayer: "With [Joseph and Nicodemus], I too will go up to the foot of the cross; I will press my arms tightly round the cold Body, the corpse of Christ, with the fire of my love … I will unnail it, with my reparation and mortifications. … I will wrap it in the new winding-sheet of my clean life, and I will bury it in the living rock of my breast, where no one can tear it away from me, and there, Lord, take your rest! Were the whole world to abandon you and to scorn you … *serviam* (cf. Jer 2:20)! I will serve you, Lord!"[2]

- ***The apostles hide*** in the Upper Room, and Christ hides "in the cleft of the rock," to better meet the soul of every human being, his beloved (cf. Song 2:14). He loves each soul to the extreme of entering the tomb (Jn 13:1), even to the point of wanting to be embalmed with the same perfumes as the human soul (Song 4:14; Ps 45:8).

- ***And Christ departs*** to plunder the underworld. "Jesus … having become a high priest for ever after the order of Melchizedek" (Heb 6:20) "enters into the inner shrine behind the curtain … as a forerunner on our behalf" (vv. 19–20). So as not to go alone, he passes through the curtain of the underworld before passing through the curtain of heaven.

- ***The Eternal Light*** is laid in the darkness of a tomb. He who sees all enters the night of Hades (literally the place "without vision"); the Morning Star goes down to enlighten "those who sit in darkness and in the shadow of death" (Lk 1:79).

- ***The Eternal Word*** enters a great silence, the utter self-emptying, or kenosis, the ultimate consequence of the Incarnation: corpselike obedience, the greatest poverty, the paradox of the highest humility.

- ***So confess with Job***: "For I know that my Redeemer lives, / and at last he will stand upon the earth" (Jb 19:25).

- Like Joseph asking Pilate to give him the body of the Son of God, each day ask of the world the ***Eucharistic Body of Christ***: not a corpse, but living, resurrected, with his soul and divinity.

- ***As a faithful disciple***, become yourself the aroma of Christ (cf. 2 Cor 2:14) by your holiness, the spikenard ointment for "his body, that is, the Church" (Col 1:24).

- ***The body of Jesus enters the paschal Sabbath***; his soul (psyche and Spirit) "break[s] in pieces the doors of bronze / and cut[s] asunder the bars of iron" (Is 45:2); he "preach[es] to the spirits in prison" (1 Pt 3:19); he directs the patriarchs, saints, and prophets, his earthly father Joseph, and John the Baptist, his forerunner, to go before him (cf. Zec 9:11). His divinity remains united to both his body and his soul.

- ***Absolute Love is stronger than death***, his passion more relentless than the grave (cf. Song 8:6). His descent is to bring Life (cf. Dom André Louf):[3] to reduce to impotence "him who has the power of death, that is, the devil" (Heb 2:14); to destroy man's last enemy, death itself (1 Cor 15:26); to bring "life and immortality to light" (2 Tm 1:10); to preach the Good News to those held in prison (1 Pt 3:19).

- ***The tombstone is placed*** over the One who is more just than Daniel and more powerful than all lions (cf. Dn 6:16). But the stone is not the final seal on his mission:

> the last word belongs not to falsehood, but to Truth,
> not to the dead end, but to the Way,
> not to death, but to Life,
> not to hatred and abuse of power, but to Love.[4]

- ***Death is visited by the Living One***; the realm of the dead seems to swallow a corpse, but he, life itself, living and life-giving, annihilates that realm. Death expected a prisoner but found Almighty God.

- ***Man having fallen*** lower than the earth, Christ willed to descend even to hell to find him.

- "***Christ is among the dead***:

  let us die to sin, to live for righteousness.
  Christ is wrapped in a white shroud:
  let us loose the bonds of our sins
  and clothe ourselves with divine light.
  Christ is in a new tomb:

let us purify ourselves of the old leaven
and become new dough,
to be a place of rest for Christ.
Christ is in the underworld:
let us descend with him into the humility that
exalts,
so that we may rise again,
and be exalted and glorified with him,
always seeing God and always being seen by him.
...
You who are bound with the winding-sheet [of
the world], come out,
you who are in darkness,
open your eyes to the [true] light,
you captives,
let your chains fall away" (St John Damascene).[5]

- ***Like the women bringing myrrh***, let us prepare from now on the perfumes (cf. Lk 23:56) of a holy life to honor the body of Christ and meet him living. Just as with the disciples who encountered the Risen One (Lk 24:13; Jn 20), it is hard for us to understand why salvation must pass through suffering and death. Let us allow him to walk with us, let us listen as his words question us, explain the Scriptures to us, and set our hearts ablaze. Let us invite him to stay in our house and share his Eucharistic Bread so that our eyes may be fully opened, and that we may recognize him, alive and victorious forever.

LET US PRAY

You hid yourself beneath the earth, as the sun is hidden from our eyes by the night of death; but rise more radiant, O Savior!

By willingly descending beneath the earth like a dead man, O Jesus, you have raised up to the heavenly dwelling all those who had fallen.

O Word, obedient to your Father, you descended into the cruel underworld, and you have resurrected the race of mortals.

Flooded with burning tears, the Virgin laments, and her heart is torn open.

On this day, a tomb contains him who holds creation in his hand.

A stone covers him who covered the heavens with beauty.

Life sleeps and hell trembles, Adam is freed from his chains.

You have fulfilled the eternal Sabbath by granting us your most holy resurrection from the dead.

On this day, hell groans and cries out: "My power is abolished; I received a dead man like all the others, but I cannot hold him. He strips me of those who were under my dominion; I held the dead captive for centuries, but he raises them all."

Glory, Lord, to your cross and to your resurrection!

And let us pray again personally:

Dear Lord Jesus,

The Way of the Cross has become our way to life.

Thank you, eternally, for all your sufferings so patiently endured for us:

For our betrayals and for your arrest, accepted out of love for me, I repent of my sins, I give you thanks, and I adore you.

The Stone of the Anointing at the entrance to the Basilica of the Holy Sepulcher

For your chains and your false trial *accepted for me,*
Peter's denial, and mine *accepted for me,*
all the blows *accepted for me,*
your scourging and the tortures *accepted for me,*
the mockery, contempt, and spitting *accepted for me,*
your crowning with thorns *accepted for me,*
the abandonment and isolation *accepted for me,*
your long carrying of the cross *accepted for me,*
your falls *accepted for me,*
your stripping *accepted for me,*
the nails driven into your flesh *accepted for me,*
your six hours on the cross *accepted for me,*
your dehydration, suffocation, and
the bursting of your heart *accepted for me,*

O Jesus, eternity will not be enough to thank you for dying on the cross for me.

Like the prodigal son, I confess that I have sinned against heaven and against God my Father (cf. Lk 15:18), and that I am utterly incapable of saving myself. I acknowledge that by your death and sacrifice, you have paid the price of my sins for me. I beg you, come into my heart and let me enter into yours, be the Lord of my whole life.

As you gave your life, I give my life to you. I will take up my cross and follow you, not as I want to, but to follow your perfect will for my life.

In the name of Jesus by whom we are saved. Amen.

From *The Imitation of Christ*:

"My soul, above all things and in all things you must always rest in the Lord, for he is the everlasting rest of the saints. O sweetest, most loving Jesus, grant that I may rest in you above anything created; above all health and beauty, all honor and glory; above all power and dignity, all knowledge and cleverness; above all riches and abilities; above all joy and gladness, above all fame and praise; above all sweetness and consolation; above all hope and promise, above all merit and desire; above all gifts and presents you can give us or pour out upon us; above all happiness and rejoicing that the mind can grasp and feel; finally, above angels and archangels and above the whole host of heaven; above everything seen or unseen, above everything that is not you, my God.

O Lord my God, you are the sum of all good, surpassing all things; you alone are most high and most powerful; you alone are completely self-sufficient and perfect; you alone are most sweet and consoling.

You alone are most beautiful and loving, most noble and most glorious above all else; in you are found existing together in all their perfection all good things that now are or ever have been or ever will be. Thus it is that anything you give me apart from yourself, anything you reveal or promise me of yourself, is too little, too unsatisfying, for as yet I have not seen you, have not fully gained possession of you. My heart cannot find its true resting place, cannot be wholly content, until it soars above all your gifts, all that you have created, and rests in you."[6]

Our Father... Hail Mary... Glory be to the Father...

The eleventh hour

It is the eleventh hour of the day: the hour when the first Adam was judged, also on the sixth day (TB, *Sanhedrin* 38b); the hour when the workers receive at the end of the day the divine grace for which they have worked so little (cf. Mt 20:9).

Arimathea

According to Eusebius (*Onomasticon* 144), Arimathea is Ramathaim-zophim (1 Sm 1:1), the town of Samuel, who anointed Da-

vid the ancestor of the Messiah, and received him into his house (1 Sm 19:18). Joseph of Arimathea received the Messiah, the Son of David, into his "house" — his tomb is *beyt-qvura* ("house of burial"), in Aramaic. His name means "height," and, in fact, as is often shown in sacred art, the high point of his life was ascending the cross to remove the nails in Jesus' hands and receive his body.

A perfume of great price

Joseph of Arimathea and Nicodemus, two members of the Sanhedrin, probably acknowledged Jesus as the Messiah. They practice the seventh corporal work of mercy toward the Fount of Mercy, bringing a vast quantity of myrrh to the measure of their love: a hundred pounds' weight, worth about 400,000 dollars today! This substance was found, together with aloes, on the Shroud of Turin.

The entombment in iconography

Icons of the Man of Sorrows show Jesus with a lifeless body, but

يا يسوع الحياة
في قبر وضعت
يسوع
المسيح

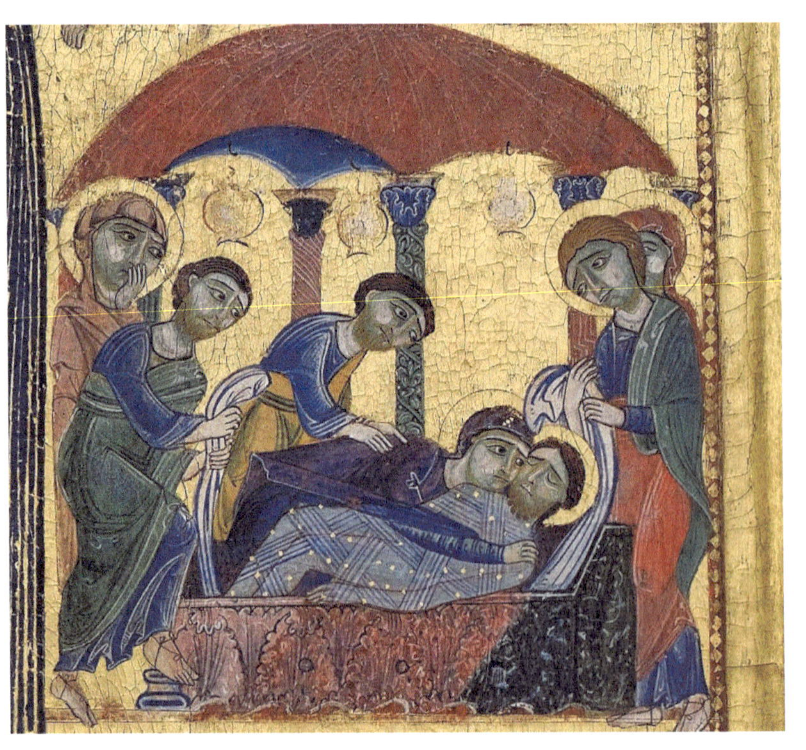

sometimes with wide open eyes, because his soul enters eternity. The traditional title is, paradoxically, "Extreme humility" (*akra tapeinôsis*), since the Son of God shows his greatness to an extreme degree by being able to descend to the lowest point of the earth and the underworld.

Sabbath and Redemption

Jewish tradition held that if Israel observed just one Sabbath perfectly, the Redemption would come through the Messiah, because this commandment was equivalent to all the commandments;[7] and, in fact, Jesus fulfilled this holy Sabbath perfectly, in the name of everyone.

Holy Saturday, the day of expectation

Christians, attuned in a special way every Saturday to the expectation of the Jewish faith, join in patient but ardent expectation of the glorious coming of the Messiah. This patience is the first of the sixteen features of love (cf. 1 Cor 13:4). Literally translated, it consists of taking a deep breath (*makrothumia*) against spiritual asthma or asphyxia. In the anamnesis at the Eucharistic consecration, the cry is "until you come again!"

Those who live faithfully through this expectation enter Mary's day, which is:

- sanctified (Gn 2:2), as Mary is "full of grace" (Lk 1:28) and all-holy (cf. Song 4:7);
- blessed by God (Gn 2:3), as Mary is blessed among all women (Lk 1:42);
- rest, as Sirach 24:12, in certain translations, says, "He who created me has rested in my tent";
- the day of many of her interventions in history, as when her veil lifted to reveal the icon of Christ every Saturday in her basilica of Blachernes (Constantinople, cf. Humbert des Romans), as when she appeared at the Rue du Bac (November 27, 1830), La Salette (September 19, 1846), Lourdes (February 13, 1858), Fátima (February 13, 1917), Syracuse (August 29, 1953), or Kibeho (November 28, 1981).

1. *Chemin de Croix*. Thirteenth Station.
2. *The Way of the Cross*, Scepter 1982.
3. Stations of the Cross for the Vatican, April 9, 2004.
4. Cf. John Paul II, Colosseum, 2000.
5. Homily for Holy Saturday, 3, 21.
6. *The Imitation of Christ*, book III, chapter 21, tr. Ronald Knox/Michael Oakley.
7. Cf. Jerusalem Talmud, *Ta'anit* 1, 10; *Shabbat* 118b.

SEVEN LAST WORDS OF CHRIST ON THE CROSS

Each of Christ's seven last words on the cross is a gift of love.

A flame to enkindle our hearts with faith, hope, and charity.

A fruit from the Tree of Life.

The testament of absolute Love.

Before Jesus, only Jacob and Moses left us their last words, to prepare for Christ. Afterward, Stephen would leave us his last words (cf. Acts 7), in the name of the Church, to continue Christ.

The word of the cross is folly to those who are perishing,
but to us who are being saved it is the power of God.
— 1 Corinthians 1:18

1.

"FATHER, FORGIVE THEM; FOR THEY KNOW NOT WHAT THEY DO."

— *Luke 23:34*

Jesus never begins by caring about himself, but rather about us, to obtain mercy for us.

The only one who has committed no offense offers himself as a victim for our offenses to be forgiven. Our victim becomes our advocate. Our sovereign high priest (cf. Heb 4:14) fulfills the eighth of his beatitudes (Mt 5:10, 44), offering his prayer for us. He who was not sent to judge the world but to save it (Jn 3:16) "overcome[s] evil with good" (Rom 12:21). He overcomes all despair, all resentment, all anger and hatred, and all bitterness.

Forgiveness is the greatest gift of all.

"They know not": Humbly, let us confess, each of us, our ignorance of the greatness of love, and our ignorance of our own sin, which so wounds God's heart, due to a blindly presumptuous and insufficient

response to divine love. It is not human knowledge that saves, but a humble response to Love come in person to save us (cf. Is 35:4).

Lift your eyes to the crucified one, let yourself be seduced by his vicarious[1] and merciful compassion, recognize him, accept his forgiveness in the Sacrament, adore him, imitate him, give your life, too, and forgive.

1. An adjective from the Latin *vicarius*, "one who takes the place of another": Christ took our place by taking upon himself the consequences of all our sins. He suffered in our place.

2.

"TRULY, I SAY TO YOU, TODAY YOU WILL BE WITH ME IN PARADISE."

— *Luke 23:43*

According to Matthew's account, the robbers crucified on either side of Jesus began by insulting him (cf. 27:44); the Greek word here is the same one used for the "robbers" who are contrasted with the Good Shepherd (Jn 10:1).

One of the robbers doubts ("Are you not the Christ?"), rejects the Father ("Save yourself!"), and seems to want to go back and take up the same life on earth as before (Lk 23:39). The other one admits his wrongdoing, confessing Jesus as Lord and King, and begging to be able to follow him.

Looking at these two robbers, or at these same two tendencies within yourself, choose between the two possible reactions to your sin, choose between life and death (cf. Dt 30:19): Right there on the cross, believe!

By contemplating the love of the crucified Christ, the one robber is converted, by a simple but true act of humility, repentance, mercy, and trust in the innocent, crucified Christ, and the condemned sinner becomes a saint, able to enter paradise that very day and be with all the other saints.

Just a few words from Christ, received in faith, turned this sinful being around. After a life spent stealing, because of his humble yet daring trust, this man ended up stealing heaven. He did not demand signs as we do. His eyes saw a cross; his heart saw a throne. And he was beatified by Mercy itself. Always hope in the all-powerful mercy of God.

If at every Mass we who die through sin say, while on our knees, inwardly, "Remember me when you come into your kingdom," Christ gives us the same response he gave to Saint Dismas. The "door of the sheep" (Jn 10:7) opens to paradise; the "word, which is able to save your souls" (Jas 1:21), and Emmanuel, through his overflowing mercy, bring about the reciprocity he is awaiting from all of us sinners.

SHORT MEDITATIONS

"Though your sins are like scarlet,
 they shall be as white as snow" (Is 1:18).

As the repentant thief asked, the Son of God remembered "his mercy" (cf. Lk 1:54).

Jacques-Bénigne Bossuet commented: "*Today*, what promptitude! *With me*, what company! *In paradise*, what repose!"[1]

> According to the apocryphal Syriac Gospel of the Infancy, the two thieves, Dismas and Gestas, were said to belong to a clan that had captured the Holy Family in Egypt but were moved by Mary's beauty to let them go.

1. *Sermon*, April 10, 1661.

EI
S: MA
RIA
ECCLA
EXALT

3.

"WOMAN, BEHOLD, YOUR SON!" … "BEHOLD, YOUR MOTHER!"

— John 19:26–27

This passage in John's Gospel reveals in particular the universal motherhood of Mary. She receives us, sinners, in exchange for Jesus, the Lord. The angel had announced to Mary that she would be the mother of the Savior; the Savior reveals to her in this "second Annunciation" that she will be the mother of all those who are redeemed.

Called "woman," she is the new "mother of all living" (Gn 3:20), the new Eve conceived without sin, without any stain of disobedience (cf Song 4:7; 5:2). She is present, and active, because she is loving.[1] Like any mother, she gives life and tenderness, she comforts and raises up … Mary is as necessary to the healthy growth of a Christian as a mother is to a child.

God chose to give us the supreme grace of the Incarnation through her; now, likewise, he wants to bring many other graces to us through

*Nineteenth-century Russian icon, on the Greek model of the icon of Extreme Humility (*akra tapeinôsis*)*

her. She is Queen and can obtain everything, the mother who can grant everything. As at the banquet of Cana, so, too, at the heavenly banquet Mary becomes the "most direct, most effective, and most loving" intercessor (cf. Cardinal Journet)[2] that we could possibly ask for. She had given birth to Christ our head (cf. Col 1:18), and here (at the foot of the cross) she was to begin to give birth to the body that we are.[3] We, "the rest of her offspring" (Rv 12:17), we, the spiritual "newborn babes" (1 Pt 2:2), can only be so by having her as our mother in heaven.

Here again, God proves his love for you: He shares with you his own mother, the most perfect creature, the one who delights him most; and loving his mother perfectly, he cannot help also loving all those he has entrusted to her as children. So, honor the mother Jesus has given you, as she deserves; love her as Christ loved her. He addressed himself here to "the disciple," who was near her; a condition, therefore, for being a genuine disciple. You, too, welcome Mary every day "into your being" (Jn 19:27, in the Greek) — that is, let yourself be formed by her as a disciple and a humble servant.

Entrust your whole life and your crosses to her so that you, too, in your flesh, may "complete what is lacking" in the passion of Christ (cf. Col 1:24).

---

1. Along these lines, the Curé of Ars said: "How she loves us! The hearts of all mothers put together are but a piece of ice in comparison!"
2. Cardinal Charles Journet, *Les Sept Paroles du Christ en Croix*, Seuil, 1952.
3. Cf. Louis-Marie Grignon de Montfort, *True Devotion to the Virgin Mary*.

4.

"MY GOD, MY GOD, WHY HAST THOU FORSAKEN ME?"

— *Matthew 27:46*

Jesus took on the whole of the human condition except sin (cf. Heb 4:15), and now he cries out all his sense of being abandoned, like you, and for you.

That extreme anguish accepted by the divine Redeemer would have been totally unimaginable in a gospel that was invented by men.

Jesus is praying Psalm 22, which, in Jewish thought, formed one indivisible whole: He already has in mind the response to God and the praise of God that saves the humiliated psalmist. Thanks to him we will never again be alone or lonely, because he is with us until the end of time (cf. Mt 28:20).

This cry is not "one of despair, but of true messianic hope."[1]

He takes upon himself all the "Whys?" we ask in times of doubt and trial. He transforms the feeling of abandonment experienced by

those who believe they have been rejected by God into a prayer of intercession with the Father.

"Why" (a search for cause and intention) can also be understood in Aramaic (*le-ma*) as:

- "To what" (what situation have you abandoned me to): absolute dereliction and total suffering, embracing all the sufferings in the history of the world.
- "For what" (in exchange for what, and for what

purpose): Jesus offers himself for the expiation of our sins (cf. Heb 2:17) and with the purpose that we would accept the redemption he is offering us.

Jesus, let my sorrows not poison me! Let them visit me as much as they must; let them make my soul desolate, fill it to the brim: I am willing, I consent in advance. But let the bitterness and distress that overwhelm me never turn into rebellion or despair. At those moments, bring me near the infinity of your agony. As I repeat in my heart the words torn from you by the excess of your suffering for humankind, may I feel my own anguish suddenly dissolve into yours like a tear dissolved into the ocean. Let my anguish cease to be selfish, let it begin to be co-redemptive.[2]

1. Journet, *Les Sept Paroles du Christ en Croix.*
2. Ibid.

5.

"I THIRST"

— John 19:28

The "living water" (Jn 4:10) is thirsty. Jesus felt abandoned by his Father, but above all, he was abandoned by men.

Physically, he is so thirsty because he "emptied himself" (Phil 2:7), even of his blood, for you.

Spiritually, the throat of the One who is a burning bush burns with desire for all those whom he has created solely out of love, but who do not know it.

God, who loves you with an everlasting, absolute love (cf. Jer 31:3), has never stopped searching for you: "Where are you?" (Gn 3:9; cf. also Song of Songs; Mt 18:10–14; and Jn 10).

The One who created oceans, clouds, glaciers, and waterfalls asks men for a drink. Since creation, God suffers without mankind. He has chosen to depend on you. He thirsts for your faith, your presence, your salvation, for *you*; he is waiting for your response! And he takes on all your desires.

Now and every day, you can quench Jesus' thirst. Console him by your conversions, your clear path of trusting God, and your compassion, shown in practical deeds, for all your contemporaries whose hearts are still dying of thirst.

Hearing these words from Jesus, Claudel responds: "Are you talking to me? Do you still need me and my sins?!"[1]

May your thirst encounter Jesus' thirst. Thirst for your redeemer, much more than for whatever is going on around you. Seek his beauty, his truth, his love. Seek him, find him, never desert him, but make his goodness and desire known to others, so that he may finally be recognized and loved.

---

1. *Le Chemin de Croix.*

*My strength is dried up
like a potsherd,
and my tongue cleaves
to my jaws.*

— Psalm 22:15

6.

"FATHER, INTO THY HANDS I COMMIT MY SPIRIT!"

— *Luke 23:46*

Jesus spoke of his Father in his first recorded words (cf. Lk 2:49); and he speaks to him in his last recorded words.

Like Jesus, through Jesus, with Jesus, and in Jesus, give everything to God the Father: projects, studies, failures, health, future, vocation, family, salvation, the time of your own death … everything.

He who breathed the breath of life into dust to create Adam now gives his Holy Spirit, the breath of eternal life. The Church is beginning to be born.

These words, referred to in Psalm 31, are said as a prayer in Judaism and Christianity every evening, just before going to sleep. The initials of the Hebrew words (*B'yad'cha Afkid Ruchi*) mean a "well" or "wellspring," the symbol of life and calmness, for that is what we hope for from God.

Let us pray with Charles de Foucauld's Prayer of Abandonment

"Father, I abandon myself into your hands;
do with me what you will.
Whatever you may do, I thank you.
I am ready for all, I accept all.
Let only your will be done in me,
and in all your creatures.
I wish no more than this, O Lord.
Into your hands I commend my soul;
I offer it to you
with all the love of my heart,
for I love you, Lord,
and so need to give myself,
to surrender myself into your hands, without reserve,
and with boundless confidence,
for you are my Father."

Into thy hand
I commit my spirit;
thou hast redeemed me, O LORD,
faithful God.

— Psalm 31:5

7.

"IT IS FINISHED"

— *John 19:30*

Jesus saves us by finishing off all that he came to do. He fulfilled or accomplished:

- God's will to save us (cf. Jn 5:30; 1 Tm 2:4);
- all the figures and prophesies of the First Covenant;
- the whole work of the new creation of the universe (Gn 2:1–2, the seventh day);
- all justice and righteousness (Mt 3:15);
- the whole of his mission;
- his holiness, or his love (Jn 13:1), whose victory will shine on Easter Sunday.

Behind his apparent failure, his (earthly) life was the most successful of all the lives ever lived, because he is the one who gave himself most

completely. He gave himself for the multitude, which included his enemies, and he is the only being in history who changed the history of the world by doing that.

In the body of the sacrificed and victorious Lamb, in the blood and water that flow from his side, everything begins.

In your turn, fulfill the purpose for which he created you and for which he let himself be killed for you. Respond to him by loving as he loved (Jn 15:12), with a sincere, disinterested gift of yourself.

JESUS UTTERED A LOUD CRY, AND BREATHED HIS LAST

— *cf. Mark 15:37*

The Redeemer of the world makes all human cries his own,
all the feelings that no mere words can express,
and he is heard (cf. Heb 5:7).
This cry of pain will become a cry of victory on Easter Day.

"And behold, the curtain of the temple was torn in two, from top to bottom …": God the Father weeps for the death of his Son; entry into heaven's sanctuary is offered to everyone; finally, the reality of divine Love taken to the extreme is revealed.

"… and the earth shook …" (Mt 27:51): the fulfillment of Sinai (cf. Ex 19:18) in Love proclaims its theophany, and death and hell tremble; concerning hardened sinners who do not confess their God the stones cry out (cf. Lk 19:40; Mt 3:9); the very rock announces the forthcoming Easter earthquake (Mt 28:2); the earth begins its exultation of joy at salvation.

LET US PRAY

Lord Jesus, I acknowledge all my sins.
You could have condemned me for my faults,
but you let yourself be condemned in my place.
Thank you for your suffering and your death on the cross.
Forgive the whole world.
Give us your Spirit
and allow me, today,
to begin a new life
in communion with you.
I want to hear your voice and follow you,
to accept my cross so that I can live with you and bring you joy.
I consecrate my whole life to you. Amen!

SALVE REGINA – HAIL, HOLY QUEEN

Hail, Holy Queen, Mother of Mercy, our life, our sweetness and our hope! To you do we cry, poor banished children of Eve. To you do we send up our sighs, mourning and weeping in this valley of tears. Turn then, O most gracious Advocate, your eyes of mercy towards us, and after this, our exile, show unto us the blessed fruit of your womb, Jesus. O clement, O loving, O sweet Virgin Mary!

Salve Regina, Mater misericordiae. Vita, dulcedo et spes nostra, salve. Ad te clamamus, exsules filii Evae. Ad te suspiramus, gementes et flentes in hac lacrimarum valle. Eia ergo, Advocata nostra, illos tuos misericordes oculos ad nos converte. Et Jesum, benedictum fructum ventris tui, nobis post hoc exilium ostende. O clemens, o pia, o dulcis Virgo Maria!

LIST OF UNCAPTIONED ILLUSTRATIONS

p. 165: Pietà, Stanisław Grocholski, 1890
p. 168: Ivory crucifix, by Joseph Villermé, ca. 1700
p. 170: Dismas, fresco by Fra Angelico (detail), San Marco, Florence, Italy
p. 174: Replica of the Antelami ambo (detail), Church of St-Germain-en-Laye, France
p. 178: Twentieth-century crucifix, Basilica of the Valle de los Caídos, Spain
p. 182: Crucifix, unknown origin and date
p. 186: Crucifix in the convent at Sovere, Italy
p. 192: Señor de los Milagros, Reynaldo, Church of María Madre de Dios, Callao, Peru
p. 194: Pietà, Juan de Avalos, 1952, Basilica of the Valle de los Caídos, Madrid, Spain
p. 199: Fresco, Bellinzona, Switzerland